D0148832

ACTION!

ACTION!

Acting for Film and Television

Robert Benedetti

Allyn and Bacon

Boston • London • Toronto • Sydney • Tokyo • Singapore

Vice President, Editor-in-Chief: *Karen Hanson*
Series Editor: *Karon Bowers*
Series Editorial Assistant: *Jennifer Becker*
Composition Buyer: *Linda Cox*
Manufacturing Buyer: *Megan Cochran*
Cover Administrator: *Linda Knowles*
Production Administrator: *Rosalie Briand*
Editorial-Production Service: *Nesbitt Graphics, Inc.*
Electronic Composition: *Publisher's Design and Production Service*

Copyright © 2001 by Allyn & Bacon
A Pearson Education Company
160 Gould Street
Needham Heights, MA 02494

Internet: www.abacon.com

All rights reserved. No part of the material protected by this copyright notice may
be reproduced or utilized in any form or by any means, electronic or mechanical,
including photocopying, recording, or by any information storage and retrieval
system, without the written permission of the copyright owner.

Library of Congress Cataloging-in-Publication Data
Benedetti, Robert L.
     ACTION! : acting for film and television / by Robert Benedetti.
        p.   cm.
     Includes index.
     ISBN 0-205-31980-7
     1. Motion picture acting.   2. Television acting.   I. Title.
     PN 1995.9. A26 B46 2000
     791.43'028—dc21   00-056552

Printed in the United States of America

10 9 8 7 6 5   08 07 06

CONTENTS

FIGURES

EXERCISES

PREFACE

When I wrote the first edition of *The Actor at Work* thirty years ago, I was teaching at Carnegie-Mellon University. Despite our frequent collaboration with public television station WQED, it never occurred to any of us to offer formal classes in acting for the camera. The situation was the same when I became Chairman of the Acting Program at the Yale Drama School. Even later, when I moved to the California Institute of the Arts as Dean of the School of Theatre, we offered no courses in film acting, despite the fact that our students frequently acted in films made by students of the School of Film and Video. As far as I know, not one of the burgeoning professional actor training programs of the sixties and seventies offered significant actor training for the camera; we all dreamt of the rosy future of repertory theatre in America and disdained training for the "commercial" world of film and television.

By the late eighties, the retrenchment of the American repertory theater movement had greatly reduced the opportunities for stage actors in America. At the same time, the expansion of television and film production drew more and more actors away from the stage. By 1990, most of the wonderful repertory theater actors with whom I had worked in the seventies and eighties had come to Los Angeles to try their luck. At this same time, I abandoned my twenty-five-year career as a teacher of acting and, with the help of former students (most notably Ted Danson) started producing films. By observing the work of a number of accomplished film actors (some of whom are quoted on the back cover), I began to appreciate first-hand the unique demands the camera makes on actors.

My experience as a producer has convinced me that our schools cannot go on pretending that film and television are not the major employers of actors in this country; a glance at the union membership numbers proves it. There is a real need for systematic, no-nonsense training for the camera wherever acting is taught in this country. This book was written to help address that need. It uses the same approach I have employed over the eight editions of *The Actor at Work*: to define underlying principles, present them in a logically sequential program of development, and provide experiential exercises that help the student to discover and internalize them for herself or himself.

My thanks to those who reviewed this manuscript, George Judy, Florida State University; Matt Tomlanovich, Southern Methodist University; and Nancy Silva, American River College. Thanks also to the fine people at Allyn & Bacon with whom I have now published several books, especially Karon Bowers.

ABOUT THE AUTHOR

For the past ten years, Robert Benedetti has been a film and television producer. He recently won Emmy awards for the HBO films, *Miss Evers' Boys* and *A Lesson Before Dying.* The latter also won a Peabody Award in 2000. Benedetti received a Ph.D. from Northwestern University. He taught acting at Carnegie-Mellon University and York University in Toronto, was Head of the Acting Department at the Yale Drama School, and was Dean of the School of Theatre at the California Institute of the Arts. He was a master teacher at Australia's National Institute of Dramatic Art and at the National Theatre School of Canada. He has directed at numerous theatres and festivals, including the Tyrone Guthrie Theatre, the Melbourne Theatre Company, and the Oregon Shakespeare Festival. His book, *The Actor at Work* has for twenty-five years been a best-selling acting text and is now in its eighth edition. He also wrote *The Director at Work* and recently published *The Actor in You.* In 2001, a new book, *Prep/Shoot/Post: An Introduction to Film and Television Production,* will be published by Allyn and Bacon.

PART ONE

Working with the Camera

INTRODUCTION

Getting Started

This book is divided into two parts. The first is "Working with the Camera," a no-nonsense, step-by-step guide to the process and techniques of shooting a film or television show. The second is "Preparing Yourself and Your Role," which presents the principles of acting for film and television, including detailed instructions for creating the inner life of a character.

Throughout, I will give examples from one of the sample scenes to be found in Appendix A: the first is a scene from Arthur Miller's great play, *Death of a Salesman*; the second is a scene from the Emmy Award-winning HBO film, *Miss Evers' Boys*; the third is a scene from the popular sitcom, *Cheers*. All three scenes should be read early on. *Miss Evers' Boys* and *Death of a Salesman* are widely available for rental on video, and I encourage you to view them in their entirety. (There were two film versions of *Death of a Salesman*; the first in 1951 starring Fredric March, and another in 1985 starring Dustin Hoffman; either is good for our purpose.)

Terms commonly used in film and television are **boldface** when they first appear. These terms, and many others, appear in the Glossary at the back of the book.

A Scene of Your Own

It will be important for you to apply what you learn to actual performance, and I advise that you select one scene of your own that you will use for all the various exercises throughout this book. You will need a partner, and together you should choose the scene, or a portion of a scene, that will serve each of you well. The scene may be drawn from a screenplay or television script, though realistic material written for the stage will also serve. Here are some qualities of a good scene for our purpose:

1. It should be *realistic* and *contemporary*, written in language that is comfortable for you.
2. It should be *close to you in age and body type*, something in which you realistically might be cast.
3. It should be *short*, capable of being read aloud in about four minutes or less.
4. Best of all, it should be a scene that *touches* you personally in some way.

If, for the sake of length, you choose to do only a portion of a scene, select a section that has a satisfying dramatic shape. It should center on some important choice faced by one of the characters.

There are many anthologies of scenes from plays, films, and television on the market; a list of useful scene sources appears in Appendix B. Whatever the source of your scene, it is important that you *read the entire play or script* from which the scene comes so that you have all the necessary information about your character and the function of the scene within the story.

Your Own Camera System

When I was in sixth grade, my school in Chicago offered piano lessons during lunch hour twice a week. Unfortunately, the school had only one piano for the fifteen students in the class. Each day, one of us would play the real piano; the rest "played" cardboard keyboards that we laid on our desks. It was, to say the least, not an effective way of learning to play the piano. Too often actors are asked to learn camera acting in pretty much the same way, without an actual camera or a chance to see the results of their efforts on screen. To avoid this, almost all of the exercises in this book will assume the availability of a rudimentary camera system.

Fortunately, recent reductions in the price of video equipment make it possible for almost anyone to gain experience in front of a camera. You will need a simple video camera, one that either contains its own cassette or feeds a video cassette recorder (VCR). Cost will determine what kind of camera you buy, but the crucial requirement is that playback be easy and instantaneous. The cheapest one-half inch VHS system has the advantage of being playable in almost any home VCR and is entirely adequate for our needs, though Hi 8 digital cameras give better quality and are now almost as inexpensive. You will need a monitor, and a seventeen-inch or larger home television set will serve well. The camera should be mounted on a tripod, and it should have a directional microphone, as most do.

A somewhat dark neutral background is useful, as is rudimentary general lighting that minimizes shadows on the actors' faces. This needn't require more than a few light sources as today's video cameras operate well at very low light levels.

A simple and reliable system is better than a more complicated one as our aim is the easy and quick recording of your work as an actor, not technical quality or visual effects. In some circumstances, it may be possible to utilize two cameras to give two "angles" on a scene or two different "shot sizes," but this is by no means essential. A rudimentary editing system would be useful in some of the later exercises but is not essential.

Familiarize yourself thoroughly with the operation of your camera and the rest of the system. If you are in a group, you will have the opportunity to serve one another as crew. Each of you should compile your own cassette containing your exercises and scene work. The recordings should be saved as they will be useful to review past work.

An important part of your development as a film actor is to become comfortable in front of the lens, and you should strive to get as much time on camera as possible. Besides doing the exercises in this book, take every opportunity to act in student and independent films and videos and to experiment on your own.

1 Training for the Camera

It is difficult for today's actor to build a viable career in live theater alone. In fact, the theatrical actors' union, Actors' Equity Association (AEA), has about 35,000 members nationwide while the Screen Actors' Guild (SAG) boasts a membership of 96,000. Simple arithmetic shows that the great majority of American actors work *exclusively* in film or television.

Despite this fact, opportunities for systematic film training remain rare outside of professional classes offered in a few large cities. Many college and university drama departments offer no classes in film acting, or at most a class or two offered near the end of the training sequence. This is partly because of the logistical and economic difficulties of providing space and equipment for such classes, but it is also a matter of philosophy: many acting teachers believe that training for the live stage is also the best preparation for the film actor and that separate classes for the camera are unnecessary. I have heard some of these teachers say that a well-trained stage actor can make the necessary adjustment to the camera "in one day."

There is some truth to this view. The fundamental principles of naturalistic stage acting are indeed a useful, even necessary, foundation for the camera actor. However, even though the basic principles of stage and film acting are similar, there are some very important differences. Not all approaches to stage acting are equally useful for the camera, and conversely the techniques of film acting are rarely successful on the stage. There are competent stage actors who never successfully make the transition to the camera and famous film actors who are hopelessly lost on a live stage.

To be most useful for the camera, an actor's training must teach him or her to find a rich and specific understanding of the inner life of the character, focusing the actor's awareness fully on internal, not external, matters. It must also encourage the actor to personalize the performance through the involvement of his or her own personality, history, and subconscious. Finally, this training must help the actor to prepare and work quickly with a minimum of rehearsal since that is how most movies and television shows are made. Live theater training does not necessarily provide all these essential skills.

Moreover, some stage techniques and habits are actually destructive in front of the camera. The actor making the transition from stage to screen must often "unlearn" a great deal. It is said that when Sir Ralph Richardson, already an acclaimed British stage actor, did his first film scene, he eagerly asked his director how it had gone. The director, who was standing behind the camera, answered, "It was all right, Ralph, except that I could hear you." Richardson's ability to project vocally and physically in a live theatre had to be modified for the camera, and the "size" of his performance had to be greatly reduced.

This adjustment in scale is one of the most common problems facing actors making the transition from stage to screen. It involves much more than simply being "smaller"; it requires an enhancement of inner richness, intensity, and specificity at the same time that external behavior is greatly economized. This requires a change in approach and personal discipline, and the actor is rare who can do this instinctively or quickly.

In this book, I will present a complete and self-contained approach to the principles, techniques, and vocabulary of film and television acting. This approach is based on the work of the great Russian director and teacher Konstantin Stanislavsky. His approach has proven especially effective for the camera, and my version of it has developed over thirty years of teaching and eight editions of my book *The Actor at Work*. I have further adapted it for film and television based on ten years of experience as a film and television producer.

Acting on Stage and on Camera

There is a fundamental difference between acting on the stage and for the camera, a difference that is deeper than technique. It is rooted in two facts: first, film is not an interactive medium; second, a camera sees differently than does a live audience. Let's consider each.

First, an actor in front of a live audience is performing *for* and *with* that audience; theater is an *interactive* situation, and the stage performance actually exists *between* the actor and the audience. The film performance, on the other hand, does not exist between the actor and the camera because the camera does not supply the kind of active reaction of the live audience. So while the stage performance is incomplete without the audience, *the film performance must be an independent reality*—it must be complete unto itself, something which the camera only "happens" to see. In fact, the goal of the film actor is not to create a performance at all, but rather a reality to be recorded and shaped by the camera as controlled by the director, director of photography, and editor.

Second, the camera sees more acutely than can any theater audience. Not only is the camera often closer than we allow ourselves to be even in real life, but it also has an infinite capacity to record microscopic details of behavior that are far from conscious control. The camera sees *into* you and responds to your thought processes in an almost analytical way. As film pioneer D. W. Griffiths once said, "the camera can photograph thought." The camera sees inner thoughts and feelings so well that in film, the inner life of the character often is of far greater importance than his or her external actions.

For example, during an important speech by a character, the film director and editor will usually choose to linger on the reaction of the listener rather than the action of the speaker. In our sample scene from *Miss Evers' Boys*, for instance, the entire scene hinges around the moment when Nurse Evers realizes that the doctors intend to let her patients die, a moment that is registered with a minimum of external movement and a maximum of internal anguish. That moment of reaction, more assuredly than any other moment in the scene, will be shot in close-up.

In sum, we can say that the stage actor functions mainly through *activity*, while the film actor functions mainly through *thought* and *feeling*.

The Film Actor's Consciousness

In the theater, Stanislavsky spoke of "dual consciousness," by which he meant how the actor's stage concerns are held simultaneously with the character's thoughts and feelings. This ability to function on more than one level at a time, maintaining artistic control through "actor awareness" while simultaneously experiencing the thoughts and feelings of the character, is essential to stage acting. A student of Stanislavsky's discovered this during an exercise:

> I divided myself, as it were, into two personalities. One continued as [the character], the other was an observer. Strangely enough this duality not only did not impede, it actually promoted my creative work. It encouraged and lent impetus to it.[1]

On the live stage this actor's awareness can never disappear altogether; it is the source of artistic control and shapes the performance as the response of the audience is felt. Some kinds of film and television situations are similar to live theater (such as, sitcoms which are performed in front of live audiences) and encourage the same sort of actor's awareness; But in general, film acting requires that *the actor's awareness must be suppressed entirely in favor of a complete involvement in the character's consciousness.*

---

[1]Konstantin Stanislavsky, *An Actor's Handbook,* trans. and ed. Elizabeth Reynolds Hapgood (New York: Theatre Arts Books, 1936), p. 9. Copyright © 1936, 1961, 1963 by Elizabeth Reynolds Hapgood.

There are several reasons why the actor's awareness is more accept-able in the theater than before the camera. In the theater, the audience is at some distance and cannot always see the tiny manifestations of actor aware-ness; even when they do, they tend to accept and ignore them because of the unspoken agreement called "the willing suspension of disbelief." The camera, however, is not so forgiving; it refuses to suspend its disbelief. It demands complete personal reality from the actor and subjects that reality to acute scrutiny.

Film audiences likewise take the film image as literally true. When Michael Douglas was playing a detective in a long-running television show, for instance, he was once excused from a traffic ticket by a policeman who took him as "one of our own." Because of this assumption that film image is completely real in even the most minute detail, it is dangerous for the film actor to manifest any awareness while performing except the immediate and entirely personal consciousness of the character. Any thought outside the character's consciousness may be seen by the camera and will seem false. This is what we mean when we say the camera requires "no acting" at all. *The camera provides the ultimate lie detector test.*

Since it is the actor's awareness that controls and evaluates the perfor-mance, film actors become extremely vulnerable when they must surrender it. For this reason, it is possible for perfectly competent film actors to give dreadful performances if they do not receive proper guidance; they depend on their director much more than do stage actors (this explains why it is so dangerous for film actors to direct themselves).

In actual practice, of course, it is nearly impossible for film actors to divest themselves entirely of their actor awareness, but it is the ideal toward which they must strive. Most film actors meet this challenge by preparing such a rich and engrossing inner life for their character that it consumes all their consciousness, and they surrender as much of their actor awareness to it as they can. We will examine inner creative technique in Part Two, but first you should come to understand the process by which films and television shows are made and the unique demands this process makes on the skills and techniques of the film actor.

Summary

Although the great majority of American actors work *exclusively* in film or television, our schools offer few opportunities for formal film training. The fundamental principles of naturalistic stage acting are indeed a useful, even necessary, foundation for the camera actor, but there are fundamental differ-ences in the two disciplines. First, film is not an interactive medium, and sec-ond, a camera sees differently than does a live audience. The camera sees inner thoughts and feelings so well it demands complete personal reality from the actor and subjects that reality to acute scrutiny. Because the camera can "photograph thought," any thought outside the character's consciousness may be seen by the camera and will seem false. This is what we mean when we say the camera requires "no acting" at all. *The camera provides the ultimate lie detector test.* In sum, we can say that the stage actor functions mainly through *activity,* while the film actor functions mainly through *thought* and *feeling.*

2 How a Film Is Organized

There are two main camera formats in common use: the multiple-camera and the single-camera. The multiple-camera format offers the advantage of speed and lower cost since large sections of material can be shot at one time, but it has many critical limitations, and its use is restricted to television sitcoms and soap operas; it will be discussed in Chapter 7. The single-camera format is much slower and more costly than the multiple-camera, but it allows much greater creative control and artistry, both for the camera and for the performer. It is used in almost all theatrical (also called feature) films, as well as movies made for television (called **MOWs** as in "Movie of the Week") and episodic television dramas such as *ER* or *NYPD Blue*. The single-camera format will be the main focus of this book.

From the actor's point of view, the process of making single-camera films is quite different from any other form of performance. The most striking difference is that a film is shot piecemeal, each scene or portion of a scene rehearsed, staged and shot at one time, though seldom in chronological sequence. To understand this unique aspect of film acting, you must first understand how the shooting of a film is organized.

In the most general terms, the production of all films is divided into three periods: the preparation, or **Prep,** the **Shoot** itself, and the period of post-production, or **Post.** The overall length of the production period is determined by the type of show being made and the size of the total budget. For instance, one-hour episodic television dramas like *Law and Order* or *The West Wing* have a budget of anywhere from just under one to over two million dollars per episode. An episode will be shot in six days or so, completing about eight or nine script pages a day (one page of standard-format script provides about one minute of finished program time). While one episode is shooting, another will be in Prep and another will be in Post.

The average television movie has a budget of between three and ten million dollars and a production schedule of about sixteen weeks. Of these, the Prep will take four or five weeks, the Shoot four weeks, and the Post six to eight weeks. A typical MOW will be shot in eighteen to twenty-four days, and about four to five pages of script will be shot each day.

A theatrical film made by a major studio has a much larger budget, ranging from twenty to two hundred million, and a correspondingly longer schedule. It will Prep and Post for months and shoot for sixty or more days, completing only a page or two of script each day. Independently financed (that is, non-studio) feature films, however, are often made with budgets and schedules similar to those of television movies, and occasionally these "indies" are made for much less. The popular independent feature *The Brothers McMullen*, for instance, was made for $24,000.

Prep

The Prep period of a single-camera film is a busy time: crews are hired, locations selected, sets, set dressing, costumes, props, and equipment planned, constructed, and procured. Visits called **scouts** are made to each location by the director, producers, and crew chiefs to discuss the shooting which will be done in each. At the same time, final casting is completed (a detailed description of the casting process appears in Chapter 14). The actors are called in for costume measurements, and, if needed, wig or makeup preparations; they may also be sent any special material needed to prepare their roles.

One of the first and most important steps in the Prep is the preparation of the **shooting script.** This carefully prepared script divides the show into scenes (numbered consecutively), each of which utilizes a single location. This script has been researched for accuracy and legal clearance has been obtained for all proper names of people and places. Any significant change in this script must be approved in advance by the director, producer, and studio or network, and the actors must keep this in mind.

Once the shooting script is completed, the first assistant director (**first AD**), **line producer** and/or unit production manager (**UPM**) prepare a day-by-day **shooting schedule.** The first step in this process is to summarize each scene in the shooting script on a colored strip of paper that indicates whether the scene is day or night, lists the cast members involved, and any special production requirements, such as rain. These strips are then slipped into a rack called the **board** (nowadays, of course, this is all done by computer) (see Figure 2.1). The strips are moved around to create the most effective shooting sequence, a process that requires a great deal of ingenuity and trial and error. The board is constantly being adjusted to reflect a host of considerations, such as the availability of locations and actors, the logistics of travel, the availability of **cover sets** to be used in case bad weather makes outdoor shooting impossible, and so on.

One of the most important factors influencing the board is the grouping of scenes into blocks that will make viable days or nights of work; film crews usually work twelve or thirteen hours a day during shooting, six days a week. If the show is being shot **on location** (that is, not on a **sound stage** but

--- END OF DAY 13 -- Mon, Oct 21, 1996 -- 3 4/8 pgs.						
5	5	INT	TUSKEGEE HOSPITAL - WARD -'32 *EUNICE IS CALLED TO BRODUS' OFFICE*	DAY	5/8 pgs.	1, 12
0	64	INT	TUSKEGEE HOSPITAL - WARD -'42/45 *PENICILLIN!!*	DAY	1 pgs.	1, 3
67	71	INT	TUSKEGEE HOSPITAL - WARD -'42/45 *BEN'S DYING.......*	DAY	2 pgs.	1, 7, 12
--- END OF DAY 14 -- Tue, Oct 22, 1996 -- 3 5/8 pgs.						
33	34	INT	TUSKEGEE HOSPITAL - BRODUS' OFFICE -'32 *THE FUNDING IS DISCONTINUED, EUNICE IS LET GO*	DAY	2 4/8 pgs.	1, 3, 4
71	75	INT	TUSKEGEE HOSPITAL - WARD -'42/45 *SHE SNEAKS IN TO GET THE PENICILLIN*	NIGHT	4/8 pgs.	1, 12
77	81	INT	TUSKEGEE HOSPITAL - WARD -'42/45 *"I KILLED HIM."*	NIGHT	1/8 pgs.	1, 3, 5
3	3	INT	TUSKEGEE HOSPITAL - WARD -'32 *BRODUS SAVES PATIENT'S LIFE*	NIGHT	2 5/8 pgs.	1, 3
--- END OF DAY 15 -- Wed, Oct 23, 1996 -- 5 6/8 pgs.						
8 A	10	INT	TUSKEGEE HOSPITAL - LOCKER ROOM -'32 *"IT'S GOING TO BE A GREAT THING"*	DAY	7/8 pgs.	1, 12
9	9	INT	TUSKEGEE HOSPITAL - BRODUS' OFFICE -'32 *THEY DISCUSS THE SYPHILIS PROGRAM*	DAY	4/8 pgs.	1, 3, 4
51	50	INT	TUSKEGEE HOSPITAL - BRODUS' OFFICE -'32 *SPINAL TAP? BACK SHOTS!*	DAY	1 2/8 pgs.	1, 3, 4
53	52,54,56PT	INT	TUSKEGEE HOSPITAL - CLINIC -'32 *WILLIE GETS HIS "TAP"*	DAY	2 4/8 pgs.	1, 4, 6
--- END OF DAY 16 -- Thu, Oct 24, 1996 -- 5 1/8 pgs.						
5 A	6	INT	TUSKEGEE HOSPITAL - BRODUS' OFFICE *"I WANT YOU TO GO MEET SOMEBODY"*	DAY	4/8 pgs.	1, 3
62	66	INT	TUSKEGEE HOSPITAL - BRODUS' OFFICE -'42/45 *"PENICILLIN!" "NO! IT COULD KILL 'EM!"*	DAY	2 1/8 pgs.	1, 3
76	80	EXT	TUSKEGEE HOSPITAL -'42/45 *AMBULANCE ARRIVES WITH HODMAN*	NIGHT	1/8 pgs.	1, 5
78	82	INT	TUSKEGEE HOSPITAL - MORGUE -'42/45 *"YOU KNOW WHAT YOU DID?" "I'D DO IT AGAIN!"*	DAY	1 2/8 pgs.	1, 3, 5
80	84PT	INT	TUSKEGEE HOSPITAL - CLINIC -'42/45 *DR.DOUGLAS HAS SEEN RUBY BLUE!!*	DAY	1 1/8 pgs.	1, 4, 6
81	84PT	INT	TUSKEGEE HOSPITAL - HALL & STAIRS -'42/45 *WILLIE TRIES THE THE STAIRS STEP*	DAY	2/8 pgs.	6
--- END OF DAY 17 -- Fri, Oct 25, 1996 -- 5 3/8 pgs.						
SATURDAY & SUNDAY OCTOBER 26 & 27 - COMPANY IDLE						
38	40	I/E	GOVERNMENT CAR -'32 *"FIRST TIME IN WASHINGTON?"*	DAY	2/8 pgs.	3, 4
39	41	EXT	FEDERAL BUILDING -'32 *CAR PULLS UP, THEY GET OUT & WALK IN*	DAY	2/8 pgs.	3, 4
●	42	INT	FEDERAL BUILDING - STAIRCASE - 33 *MONEY DRIED UP - "COOL DRINK?"*	DAY	6/8 pgs.	3, 4, 13, 14, 15
37B	43	INT	FEDERAL BUILDING - STAIRCASE - 33 *HIPPOCRATIC OATH v. FUNDING*	DAY	7/8 pgs.	3, 4

FIGURE 2.1   A Page from a Board. The sample scene from *Miss Evers' Boys* is listed as Scene 66 on Day 17. This and the other documents from *Miss Evers' Boys* reproduced here were prepared by first AD James Griffin and UPM Derek Kavanagh.

in a real place) a host of other considerations come into play. Putting a film company on location is very much like mounting a military operation, especially when shooting occurs in a remote location. When using real locations, the company will probably have to move from place to place. These *company moves* take precious time out of the schedule, so all the scenes needed in a given location will be shot before the company leaves that location and moves to another, regardless of the sequence in which those scenes appear in the script.

When the board has begun to take shape, the proposed shooting sequence is laid out as a "day out of days" (**D-O-O-D**) that lists each cast member and indicates when he or she will start work (SW), work (W), be **on hold** (H) and finish working (FW) (see Figure 2.2). This document is called a "day out of days" because it correlates the days of shooting to the working days of the actors. A separate D-O-O-D is also prepared for vehicles, animals, special effects, and other elements of the production. The D-O-O-D will reveal the need to make further changes in the board in order to consolidate the work period of certain actors, to allow time for changes in makeup and costume (which can take many hours), to take into account the need for extras and special equipment, and so on.

As planning continues during the weeks of Prep, changes are continuously being made to the board and usually continue to be made throughout the shooting period. Sometimes changes must be made at the very last minute as conditions change, and new boards, each on a different color of paper, are published.

Near the end of the Prep, when the board and D-O-O-D are somewhat stable, a shooting schedule is published which contains complete details of everything needed to complete the work planned for each day. This complete schedule is also published in a simplified form called the one-line shooting schedule, or "**one-liner**" (see Figure 2.3).

You see that organizing a film shoot is like building a complex "house of cards" in which every change affects the whole arrangement and can have enormous financial impact. Unfortunately, the artistic needs of the actors, which have relatively little impact on the budget, are usually the lowest priorities influencing this process.

As a result of all these economic and logistical considerations, the scenes in a film are almost always shot out of chronological sequence, even to the extent that emotionally climactic scenes may sometimes be shot before the scenes which prepare for those climaxes. This, more than any other single factor, makes very special demands on you as an actor. A strong understanding of the progression and emotional arc of the role must guide you in providing each scene, and each shot within each scene, with its proper content and tone. You must prepare each shot taking into account what will have gone before and what will follow, and how it will fit into the emotional and psychological progression of the character throughout the entire film.

"MISS EVERS' BOYS"

Report created Sat, Oct 5, 1996

October	7	8	9	10	11	12	13	14	15	16	17	18	19	20	21	22	23	24	25	26	27	28	29	30	31	1	Rehearse	Travel	Work	Hold	Holiday	Loop	Start	Finish	TOTAL
Day of Month	7	8	9	10	11	12	13	14	15	16	17	18	19	20	21	22	23	24	25	26	27	28	29	30	31	1									
Day Of Week	M	Tu	W	Th	F	Sa	Su	M	Tu	W	Th	F	Sa	Su	M	Tu	W	Th	F	Sa	Su	M	Tu	W	Th	F									
Shooting Days	1	2	3	4	5	6		7	8	9	10	11	12		13	14	15	16	17	18		19	20	21	22	23									
1. Miss Evers	S	W	W	W	W	W		W	W	W	W	W	W		W	W	W	W	W	W		H	W	W	W	WF			22				10/7	11/1	23
2. Caleb	S	W	W	W	W	W		W	H	W	W	W	WF																11	1			10/7	10/19	12
3. Dr. Brodus												S	W		W	W	H	W	W	W		W	W	WF					10	1			10/18	10/30	11
4. Dr. Douglas												S	W		H	H	W	H	W	W		W	W	WF					8	3			10/18	10/30	11
5. Hodman					S	W		W	H	W	H	W	W		H	H	W	H	W	H		H	H	W	W	WF			11	8			10/11	11/1	19
6. Willie					S	W		W	H	W	H	W	W		H	H	W	H	W	H		H	W	W	W	WF			12	7			10/11	11/1	19
7. Ben					S	H		H	H	W	H	W	W		H	H	W	H	W	H		H	H	W	H	WF			8	11			10/11	11/1	19
8. Mr. Evers	S	W	WF																										3				10/7	10/9	3
9. 1st Senator																							SWF						1				10/28	10/29	1
10. 2nd Senator																							SWF						1				10/28	10/29	1
11. 3rd Senator																							SWF						1				10/28	10/29	1
12. Betty Parsons															SWF														1				10/21	10/21	1
13. Dr. Larkin																						SWF							1				10/28	10/28	1
14. Dr. Davis																						SWF							1				10/28	10/28	1
15. Dr. Hamilton																						SWF							1				10/28	10/28	1
16. Old Man #1										SWF																			1				10/14	10/16	1
17. Announcer															SWF														1				10/2	10/2	1
18. Nurse - Sc. 68						SWF																							1				10/12	10/12	1
19. PATIENT #1 - Sc. A20											SWF																		1				10/17	10/17	1
20. PATIENT #2 - Sc. A20												SWF																	1				10/18	10/19	1

FIGURE 2.2   A Day-Out-of-Days. The sample scene from *Miss Evers' Boys* appears on shooting day 17.

17

MISS EVERS' BOYS

Shooting Schedule

Fri, Oct 4, 1996

SHOOT DAY #16 -- Thu, Oct 24, 1996

Scene #6 | **INT - TUSKEGEE HOSPITAL - BRODUS' OFFICE -'32 - DAY** | 4/8 Pgs.

"I WANT YOU TO GO MEET SOMEBODY"

Cast Members   **Props**   **Set Dressing**
1. Miss Evers   keys   Large county map W/ pins
3. Dr. Brodus   Practical sink.

Scene #34 | **INT - TUSKEGEE HOSPITAL - BRODUS' OFFICE -'32 - DAY** | 1 2/8 Pgs.

THE FUNDING IS DISCONTINUED.

Cast Members   **Set Dressing**
1. Miss Evers   Practical sink.
3. Dr. Brodus
4. Dr. Douglas

Scene #66 | **INT - TUSKEGEE HOSPITAL - BRODUS' OFFICE -'42/45 - DAY** | 1 7/8 Pgs.

"PENICILLIN!" "NO! IT COULD KILL 'EM!"

Cast Members   **Set Dressing**
1. Miss Evers   Practical sink.
3. Dr. Brodus
4. Dr. Douglas

Scene #50 | **INT - TUSKEGEE HOSPITAL - CLINIC -'32 - DAY** | 1 2/8 Pgs.

SPINAL TAP? BACK SHOTS!

Cast Members
1. Miss Evers
3. Dr. Brodus
4. Dr. Douglas

Extras
2 other doctors
5 other nurses

END OF DAY #16 - 4 7/8 Total Pages

SHOOT DAY #17 -- Fri, Oct 25, 1996

FIGURE 2.3 **A One-Liner. This is for the day the sample scene from** *Miss Evers'* *Boys* **was shot.**

Rehearsal

Even though some film directors insist on having a period of rehearsal with principal cast members before shooting actually starts, such advance rehearsal time is unusual, especially on remote locations. Because it may require actors to be brought to the location days or weeks early, it is very expensive. More often, especially in television, an actor will report to a remote location only a day or two before he or she must actually perform, with costume fittings having been done previously. When shooting is done locally, rather than on location, the actor may report only on the day he or she works.

For all these reasons, rehearsal for a film scene will usually occur only on the set just before the scene is shot. This means that you as an actor will most often have to prepare your role entirely on your own. Sometimes, you may even have to perform with very little input from the director. The best policy is to be self-sufficient when you must but eagerly open to any help you may get from your director.

Because lighting and other technical matters take so much time during shooting, the actors are often able to get together to run lines and feel their way through a scene, sometimes under the supervision of the director, sometimes not. It is a question of protocol as to whether actors should rehearse without their director present, but if it is a choice between rehearsing on your own or not rehearsing at all, I recommend rehearsing. The director will see what you have done in any case and will change it if necessary.

Film actors, by the way, do not rehearse the blocking or external movements in a scene for fear of developing a mechanical or premeditated quality. They rehearse only the lines and—for themselves individually—the inner process which lies beneath the lines. The only exceptions are fights or other physical business which may have safety implications or movements which require very precise positioning for the camera.

Handling Your Lines

It is always assumed that you will arrive on the set with your lines memorized. However, since films are shot in such small pieces, it is usually possible to begin with a general sense of the lines and do the final memorization the day before, or even on the set. On the day of shooting, a half-size copy of the script pages to be shot (called **sides**) is distributed.

Throughout the shoot, script changes may be made, sometimes even at the last minute. When this happens, new script pages containing the changes are issued. These changed pages are different colors, with the sequence of colors established by tradition (white, then blue, pink, yellow, and so on). On each new page, the changed lines will be marked with an asterisk in the margin. (By the time the show has been shot, many colors of paper will have been used, and the completed script is called a **rainbow**.) Changed pages are sometimes distributed on the set just before shooting. It is no wonder that film actors tend to put off final memorization as long as possible.

Sometimes actors will suggest extensive rewriting of lines. In such extreme cases the changes must be discussed at least one day or more before the scene is scheduled, since significant changes must be approved in advance by the network, studio, or other financing entity. More often, lines are changed only slightly by the actor to personalize them or to make them more comfortable in the mouth. The latitude given to the actors to make such changes varies, depending on the attitude of the director and producers. (Much to their chagrin, writers are almost never present during shooting except in episodic television and sitcoms, where the writers are often also the producers.)

Slight changes in the script also occur because film actors learn their lines somewhat more "loosely" than do stage actors. Stage actors, after all, are memorizing so as to repeat the performance eight times a week indefinitely, while film actors are striving for that one spontaneous moment after which the director will say "cut and print." The high degree of spontaneity and authenticity required by the camera encourages the film actor to hold his or her lines loosely in the memory so that they must be truly "rediscovered" each time the scene is shot. Some film actors say they like to "learn the action, not the words." In any case, the words should be held just as a swordsman is taught to hold a sword, "like a little bird; not so tightly that you strangle it, not so loosely that it flies away."

Here, for example, is a speech from our sample scene in *Miss Evers' Boys* as written:

> Some chronic syphilitics have a fatal allergic reaction to penicillin . . . called the Herxheimer reaction. It's been proved. Washington is researching the question, to determine the degree of risk.

Here is the same speech as delivered by the actor, with the changes indicated:

> Some chronic syphilitics *suffer* a fatal allergic reaction to penicillin . . . *It's* called the Herxheimer reaction. *Now,* it's been *proven.* Washington is *doing a study right now* to determine the degree of risk.

Assuming that slight changes like these are allowed, they are recorded by the **script supervisor** during the first take. It is necessary that in subsequent takes the words match the first to allow for editing, and the script supervisor will correct you if you go astray. The script supervisor is responsible for **continuity** and makes sure that it will be possible to cut from take to take with everything matching: the words, your position (whether your right hand was over the left or vice versa), the amount of water in your glass and on which words you drank, *everything* down to the smallest detail. This requires tremendous powers of observation and memory by the script supervisor, since hours and perhaps even days may elapse between one take and another in a given scene. You will depend on the script supervisor a great deal for help in all these matters.

In situations when time for line memorization is extremely limited (as when hosting an event or when extensive rewriting has been done at the last minute) or if the lines contain complex technical information that must be said correctly, **teleprompters** or **cue cards** may be used to help you with your lines. Some videotaped auditions, especially those for commercials, will also use cue cards. The trick to using these successfully is to move your eyes as little as possible as you read, using as much of your peripheral vision as you can. But in all, this is a special skill you're better off not having to learn; instead, practice learning lines quickly.

Summary

The most striking difference between stage and film is that a film is shot piecemeal, each scene or portion of a scene rehearsed, staged, and shot at one time, though seldom in chronological sequence. The production of all films is divided into three periods: the preparation, or Prep, the Shoot itself, and the period of post-production, or Post. One of the first and most important steps in the Prep is the preparation of the shooting script. Once it is completed, the individual scenes are arranged in a logical shooting sequence on the board and laid out as a day out of days that lists when each cast member will work. Eventually, a shooting schedule and a one-line version is published that contain complete details of the work planned for each day. Organizing a film shoot is like building a complex "house of cards" in which every change affects the whole arrangement.

Rehearsal for a film scene will usually occur only on the set just before the scene is shot, and it is assumed that you will arrive on the set with your lines memorized. This means that you will most often have to prepare your role entirely on your own.

As you can see, a film actor's work is affected by many logistical and technical considerations, and preparation time is extremely limited. Your best defense against these many distractions and the inevitable pressures of a movie set is *thorough mental preparation,* especially a clear sense of the inner life and arc of the role, and of the structure and function of each scene and each part of each scene. You will learn the techniques necessary to accomplish this in Part Two.

3 How a Single-Camera Film Is Made

Once shooting is underway, each day's work is announced on a **call sheet.** It is distributed at the end of each day of shooting and lists the following day's work in shooting sequence, with the **call** (the time when people must report to the set) for each department (see Figure 3.1). Although the intention is to stick to the sequence of work planned on the board and one-line schedule, last minute changes are often required by unforeseen factors like unfinished work being carried forward or bad weather. This means that you will sometimes not know exactly what is to be shot on a given day until the call sheet is published, twelve hours in advance.

Union regulations require that under most circumstances actors must have at least twelve hours off between calls (on location this must include travel time to and from the set with transportation provided). This is called the **turnaround.** If an actor's turnaround must be broken, they must give their permission and are paid a handsome penalty.

The day of shooting begins when you report for your call, receive your wardrobe, and perhaps make an initial visit to the hair and makeup department. You are then called to the **set** to go through the scene to be shot with the director and the director of photography (called the **DP**).

On the set, you will usually read through the scene, then walk it through. In this process, called the **line-up,** the director, actors, and DP will work out the positioning of the characters in the scene, called the **blocking.** Simultaneously, the director and DP are designing the camera positions: the blocking of the actors and the camera is done in relation to one another.

As the basic blocking pattern is developed, a member of the camera crew sets the **marks,** colored pieces of tape (a different color for each actor) that indicate where the actor's feet are at key moments in the scene. As you do the scene, you must "hit your marks" exactly, without looking down. It can even matter which foot your weight is on, since the composition of the shot and the focus of the camera may require your head to be in a precise location at a precise time.

When the shot requires that you look at another character who is off-camera, your eyes must be placed in precisely the right place; if the **eye lines**

Miss Evers' Boys		Crew Call: 7:30 AM				Call Sheet	

Pahana Productions
1252 W. Peachtree St. Suite 100						Date: Monday, October 21, 1996	
Atlanta, GA 30309		Shooting Call: 8:30 AM				Day 13 of 23	
(404) 897-5456						Location: Kirkwood Elem School	

fax (404) 897-3545
Director: Joseph Sargent — Sunrise: 7:47 AM
Executive Producers: Robert Benedetti, Laurence Fishburne — Sunset: 6:57 PM
Producers: Derek Kavanagh, Kip Konwiser

Scenes	Set	Cast	Pages	D/N	Sequence	Location
3	INT. Hosp -Clinic '32	1 ,3	2 5/8	N2	1932	Kirkwood Elementary School
	Brodus saves patient's life.					701 Kirkwood Dr.
						Atlanta, GA 30307
50	INT. Tusk Hosp Clinic '32	1, 3, 4	1 2/8	D	1932	
	Spinal Tap ! Back Shots					
9	EXT. Tuskegee Hosp '32	1, 3, 4	7/8	D4	1932	
	They discuss the syphillis program					
* *	TIME PERMITTING	* *				
**52, 54	INT. Hosp -Clinic '33	1 ,4 ,6	(2 4/8)	D20	1933	
	Willie gets tapped.					
**56pt.	INT. Hosp -Clinic '33	1 ,6	(1/8)	D20	1933	
	Other patients have left					Nearest Hospital:
						Dekalb Medical Center
						2701 North Decatur Rd.
		Total Pgs:	4 6/8			Decatur, GA 30030
						404-501-1000

Cast - Weekly & Day Players

Character	Cast	Status	Leave	Makeup	Set Call	Remarks
Miss Evers	1. Alfre Woodard	W	6:40 A	7A	8:30 A	P/U @ Grand
Dr. Brodus	3. Joe Morton	W	7:10A	7:30A	8:30 A	P/U @ Grand
Dr. Douglas	4. Craig Sheffer	W	7:40A	8A	9A	P/U @ Grand
Hodman	5. Von Coulter	H				courtesy pick-up @ Grand
Willie	6. Obba Babatunde	W	8:40 A	9A	10A	P/U @ Grand
Ben	7. Thom Gossom, Jr.	H				courtesy pick-up @ Grand

Stand-Ins			Atmosphere		
1 Miss Evers Stand-in		@ 8:30 A	14 patients		7:30 A
1 Douglas stand-in		@ 8:30 A	5 Nurses		7:30 A
1 Brodus stand-in		@ 8:30 A	1 adolescent w/ chest bandange		7:30 A
1 Willie stand-in		@ 8:30 A	3 DOCTORS		

Advance Shooting Schedule

Special Instructions:

Props: antiseptic, bandages, false torso, needle, syringe, stethescope

Day 14	TUES. October 22				
				Grip & Elec: tent in clinic windows	
71	INT. Tuskegee Ward '42/45 N	1 , 7	2		
75	INT. Tuskegee Ward '42/45 N	1	4/8		
82	INT. Hospital Morgue '42 N	1 ,3 ,5	1 5/8	Makeup: makeup to match fake torso	
80	INT. Tuskegee Hallway '42/45 N	1 ,5	1/8		
DAY 15	WEDNESDAY OCT. 23			Wardrobe: surgical gown & mask	
5	INT. TUSKEGEE WARD '32	1 , 12	7/8		
10	INT. " "	1 , 12	7/8		
45	INT. " "	1 , 12	3 7/8		

** NO FORCED CALLS WITHOUT PRIOR APPROVAL FROM UPM **

Unit Production Manager	1st Assistant Director	2nd Assistant Director
Derek Kavanagh	James Griffin	Jonathan Watson

FIGURE 3.1   A Call Sheet.

of the various characters are not consistent in the various shots of a scene, it can't be edited together.

Once the marks have been placed and eye lines established, the director will call for the **second team.** These are the "stand-ins" who are the same height and coloration as their **first team** counterparts. They may even wear the name of their character or actor on a card around their neck. The second team repeats the blocking pattern while the DP and his lighting crew chief, the **gaffer,** adjusts the lighting. The **camera operator** and DP also set the positioning of the camera, which has its own blocking and is marked by the person who moves it, called the **dolly grip.** At each blocking position, the **focus puller** records the distance between the actor and the lens. The three people it takes to run a film camera function as one team during the take (see Figure 3.2).

All this can take hours, during which the second team is standing in for the first. Meanwhile, the first team is having the final touches put on their wardrobe, hair, and makeup. During this time they are managed by people wearing walkie-talkies, the **second AD** and the second second AD, who must be aware of each actor's whereabouts at all times. These assistants give the actors their advance warnings as the time to report to the camera approaches and make sure that the necessary wardrobe, makeup, and hair work is done on time. Since scenes are shot out of chronological sequence, the makeup,

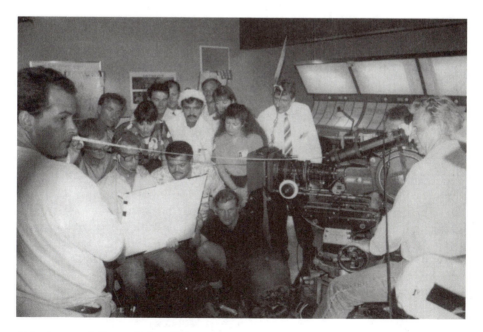

FIGURE 3.2   A Scene Being Shot.

hair, and wardrobe people check Polaroid photographs that document each character's "look" for each scene to guarantee continuity.

Shooting out of sequence makes it critical that each actor reviews the story up to the point to be shot, *especially the scene just prior.* This review will give you the proper starting point for the scene. You will also consider how the scene should end to best lead into the scene to follow.

When the lighting and camera preparations are finished, the first team is recalled to the set for shooting and is expected to report promptly, ready for work. The cardinal rule is that though everyone must wait for the camera, *the camera must never wait for anyone.*

Shooting

On the set, the first AD serves as "first officer" for the director, who is the "captain" of the ship. The first AD makes sure that everything needed for shooting is in place and that all personnel are ready. He or she communicates all logistical information leaving the director free to speak to the actors about creative matters.

At the camera, the actors assume their **first position.** Throughout the process of shooting a single-camera film, the crucial demand on you as the actor is to deliver a performance in which each moment, take after take, is both consistent and alive, despite a host of distractions. At the start of each take, the director may be suggesting adjustments in the emotional tone of the performance, the DP may be suggesting that you put your weight on your right foot, the script supervisor may be reminding you on which word you drank, the sound person may be adjusting your microphone, the makeup person refreshing your eye liner, the wardrobe person fluffing up your shirt front, and the hair person spraying fixative on your head. It is an intense, exciting, and exhausting process which makes tremendous demands on your concentration, emotional control, and grasp of the material. Your technique must be thoroughly assimilated and functioning without conscious thought, and your inner preparation for the particular role and scene must support you in keeping your priorities and dramatic intent clearly in mind.

The first shot is usually the **master,** the widest and most inclusive view of the scene. Subsequent shots, called **coverage,** are from various camera **angles.** These usually "tighter" shots of one or two actors (called **singles** and **two-shots**) will later be inserted into the master by the editor. In a later chapter we will discuss the requirements of adjusting to the position of the camera and its proximity (called **shot size,** as in "wide shot," "medium shot," "**close-up,**" and "extreme close-up").

Each segment of shooting is a **take.** Each take is often preceded by a quick check of costume and makeup, perhaps a check of the distance between the actor and the lens (the focus puller uses a tape measure for this). The director and the DP, accompanied by the script supervisor and the producers (if they are present) gather around a small video monitor behind and at a little distance from the camera. This monitor shows the **video assist** that comes directly from the camera lens as the scene is shot. This group of people is sometimes called "video village," and it is expected that everyone except the people mentioned above will stay away from the monitor during shooting out of respect for the director's need to concentrate on the scene.

When on a sound stage (rather than on location), the First AD will call **"on a bell"** and a bell rings (either literally or metaphorically) that signals everyone the take is about to start. When the set is on a bell, any air conditioning or other noisy machinery is stopped, everyone stands still and falls utterly silent (no whispering or moving, no matter how far away from the camera), and warning lights inside and outside the sound stage light up to stop anyone from entering or leaving. If the shoot is outdoors, the AD's and production assistants (PA's) are stationed at various places to hold traffic and let everyone know that "we're **rolling**." All these restrictions remain in effect until the director stops the take.

When everything is ready for the take, the First AD calls **"roll it"** and the production **sound mixer** starts the recorder. When the recorder is up to speed, the sound mixer calls **"speed"** (in our digital age this is instantaneous and merely signals that the sound mixer is ready). There is then a call for **"slate,"** and the camera operator starts the camera as the camera assistant places a **clapper board** in front of the lens to record the scene, shot, and take numbers while calling them out (as in "scene eight baker, take two"). He or she then hits the clapstick on top of the board to establish the synchronization point for sound and picture.

The take then begins when the director calls **"action,"** and ends only when he or she calls **"cut."** It is extremely important that the actors neither begin before the call of action nor stop before the call of cut. Only the director is allowed to control shooting in this way. Of course, if you or another actor forget your lines, miss a mark, or have some other inadvertent accident, you simply stop and apologize with a word or two. Only the director can stop the camera, however, so you remain ready to resume immediately.

When the take is interrupted, the director may keep the camera rolling and tell you to "pick it up from" some recent point in the scene, or the camera may be stopped and the take restarted. Each time the take is redone, the actors are sent to their opening positions by the first AD (*"back to one"*). If it is necessary to redo only a portion of the scene, it is called a **pickup.**

During each take, the production sound mixer, script supervisor, and director listen over headphones to the dialogue being recorded. The microphone may be hung from a **boom** which is held on the end of a long pole over the actors' heads, or when that is impossible, a **radio microphone** is hidden in the actor's costume and broadcasts to a receiver mounted nearby. In either case, the microphones are extremely sensitive, and it is unnecessary (and undesirable) for you to "project" as you would in a theater. Instead, you should speak exactly as you would in a real life situation, even to the point of whispering if required by the scene. When time permits, certain off-camera lines may be recorded without picture as **wild lines**.

A scene may require many shots. The sample scene from *Miss Evers' Boys*, for instance, was numbered scene 66 and required seven shots, each from a different angle and/or using a different shot size. The director, Joseph Sargent, blocked the scene so that Nurse Evers would be torn between the two doctors, who are on opposite sides of the room for much of the scene. The challenge to Director of Photography Donald M. Morgan was to light for both sides of the room simultaneously. Here is a list of the shots used to cover the scene; please reread the scene in Appendix A (see Figure 3.3).

> *Scene 66:* A "flowing master" of the entire scene starting as a single of Evers (played by Alfre Woodard) with Douglas (played by Craig Sheffer) in the background; Douglas comes forward into an over-the-shoulder two shot favoring him; the camera then follows him into a two shot with Brodus (played by Joe Morton); Douglas then returns to the two shot with Evers to deliver the bad news ("Autopsy"); finally the camera follows him back to his starting position in a medium single for his last lines.

Shot 66   **Four Positions from the Master**

"They must have penicillin!"   "I'm afraid we can't allow that."

"It's called the Herxheimer reaction."   "Autopsy"

FIGURE 3.3   A Scene from *Miss Evers' Boys*. Photos courtesy of HBO.

66A: A closer single of Douglas for his final lines of the scene.

66B: A close single of Evers from hearing the bad news through her exit. This is the crucial shot of the scene.

66C: An over-the-shoulder shot looking past Evers to Brodus at his desk; focus shifts (is "racked") as she turns to face Douglas (who has now returned to his desk behind her); Evers then exits frame and camera ends on Brodus for his last line and exit.

66D: A close single of Brodus for the entire scene.

66E: A wider single of Brodus for his opening lines.

Shot 66A

"We have a chance to make history here."

Shot 66B Two Positions from the Closeup of Evers

Her reaction to "autopsy."   Her exit.

Shot 66C   Two Positions from the Racking Shot

"That will make it science, not guess work."   "We have to wait for them to die?"

FIGURE 3.3   Continued

(continued on next page)

Shot 66D

"Let me talk to her."

Shot 66E

"Penicillin cannot undo the damage that's been done already."

FIGURE 3.3   Continued

When the director is satisfied with a take, and the DP, camera operator, and sound mixer concur that it was technically good, the director will tell the script supervisor to "**print it.**" Work then begins on the next shot. Each of the seven shots in the scene from *Miss Evers' Boys,* for example, required between one and five takes. Each time the camera is moved, it is a new **setup** and the lighting must be adjusted. The whole process continues until all the shots required to complete the scene have been made. The seven shots needed for the scene from *Miss Evers' Boys,* for example, took some six hours to shoot.

When the last shot needed for the scene is done, the AD calls "**check the gate,**" and the camera assistant looks inside the camera to be sure there was nothing amiss that might ruin the film. If it is clear, the company *moves on* to the next scene, which is a "**new deal.**" This process is repeated until the next-to-last shot of the day is reached, called the **Abby Singer** after a legendary producer. The last shot of the day is called the **martini** for obvious reasons. The end of shooting for the day is a **wrap** (as is the end of the entire production period). As you sign out at the end of the day, you receive the callsheet for the next day's work.

The film shot during the day is sent to a laboratory, often by special courier, and developed. The best takes of each shot, as identified by the director, are actually printed from the negative or transferred directly to video; the printed takes are processed overnight and the **dailies,** usually in the form of video cassettes, are delivered the next day to the director, to the editor, and to the producers. This is done so that if something has gone wrong, there may be time to **reshoot** before the company has moved on.

In any single-camera process, there is a good deal of waiting between takes for lighting and set preparation. During these waiting times you must preserve your focus and emotional energy. Film acting could be described the way I once heard a commercial pilot describe flying: endless periods of boredom punctuated by moments of sheer terror.

Post-Production: Looping

Once the Shoot is wrapped, the editor finishes assembling the dailies into the *rough cut*, also called the **first assembly.** According to the Director's Guild **(DGA)** rules, the director then has a period of time in which to refine the film to produce the *director's cut*; during this period, no one except the director and editors are allowed to see the film. The director's cut is then delivered to the producers, who always request some (or many) changes. This process can last for weeks or months, with various versions of the film bouncing back and forth between the director, editing room and the producers, and it may sometimes be decided to reshoot some material, even to the point of altering the story-line. Eventually the cut is **locked,** meaning that no further changes in the visual aspects of the film will be made.

At this point, the emphasis shifts to the audible aspects of the film. **Spotting** sessions are held at which the director, composer, editor, and **supervising sound editor** decide where music cues and major sound effects are to be placed. The supervising sound editor also reviews the production sound tapes to decide what bits of dialogue will need to be replaced. At this point you, the actor, may be called in for **looping,** also called Automatic Dialogue Replacement (**ADR**).

There are many reasons why dialogue from the original sound track (called the **production track**) may need to be replaced. Poor sound quality, background noise, or a poor line reading are the most common. On the ADR stage, you will be shown the portion of the scene to be corrected and will listen to the production track on headphones. If the section to be changed is longer than a phrase, it will have been broken into short pieces. The scene is then replayed. As the portion of dialogue to be replaced approaches, you will hear three beeps over the headphones; you then synchronize your voice to match the original, with whatever improvements or adjustments may be required. Several takes are usually necessary to achieve a final result that marries seamlessly with the production track.

Looping is a skill which can be quickly learned by most actors, and every effort is made to prepare the material in easy, "bite size" chunks. The legendary producer John Houseman once told me that Sir John Gielgud, called to loop a very long speech in Shakespeare's *Julius Caesar,* waved away the little pieces of dialogue prepared by the looping supervisor and read the entire speech in one take, synchronizing perfectly to every frame of the film.

ADR may also be used to replace lines that have been rewritten to improve the story or to account for material that has been edited out. These changed lines must be written to fit the existing mouth movements. This is not much of a problem in a wide shot, but it can be tricky business in a close-up.

To complete the preparation of the sound materials for the show, **Foley** artists (named after the person who developed the technique) produce footsteps, glass clinks, door sounds, and other specific sounds that must be synchronized to the picture. Sound editors prepare other sound effects like rain, thunder, animal and traffic noises, and so on, producing what is called the **prelay.** Groups of actors are also brought in to provide background conversations, telephone voices, and other vocal embellishments. This is called the **walla,** and such specialists are called *"looping groups."* Work in a looping group can be a meaningful and regular source of employment.

By now the composer has finished writing the music for the picture (called the **underscoring**) and this is recorded at a **scoring session** by an orchestra, usually augmented by an electronically prepared track. These tapes are carefully prepared for use by the **music editor.**

Now, with all the sound elements in hand, the director, producers, editor, composer, music editor, and supervising sound editor gather on a **dubbing stage.** Here they work with two or three mixers to blend dialogue, effects, and music to produce the **final mix** of the show.

Summary

On the day of shooting, you will arrive at your call time, receive your wardrobe, and perhaps report for preliminary makeup and hair preparation. At some point you will be called to the set to do a line-up of your scene in which you will do a run-through while the blocking will be established for you and for the camera. You are then released for final wardrobe, makeup and hair work while the second team stands in for lighting and camera preparation. Meanwhile, you may have time for additional rehearsal while the AD's keep track of you.

When the camera is ready, you report immediately and shooting begins. The director calls "action" to begin each shot, and "cut" to end it. Only the director may control shooting in this way. When he or she is satisfied with a take, and the camera and sound people have confirmed that the take was good, he or she calls "print," and everyone moves on to the next shot. This process repeats itself until the day's work is done. At the end of the day, the call sheet for the next day's work is published, and so on, until the picture is wrapped.

During Post, you may be called in to ADR lines of dialogue, and this looping becomes an element that goes into the final mix of the show.

CHAPTER

4 Shot Size

Now that you understand the process by which a film is made, you are ready to explore the specific demands the camera makes on you as an actor.

Your first concern about the camera is its proximity. The closer it is, the bigger you are within the frame; as the camera moves farther away, you become smaller. The relative distance between actor and camera, then, determines **shot size** (see Figure 4.1). The closest camera position is for an "extreme close-up" in which we can see the pores in your skin; the greatest distance is an "extreme longshot" in which you can be seen only as an element of the environment.

The camera needn't actually move to change the shot size; different lenses can have the effect of making it seem closer or farther away, and a "zoom" lens can do this with infinite variation. Though shot size could be varied almost infinitely, common usage has established six shot sizes as being the most common, as listed in Figure 4.1. Each of these shot sizes carries a different psychological implication and makes different demands on you as an actor.

Distance and Relationship

To understand the implications of different shot sizes, you must start with an understanding of how different distances operate in real life. A psychologist named Edward Hall studied people's attitudes and behaviors depending on the distance between them; he called this study "proxemics." He found that we all have a highly developed sense of psychological territory, and this is reflected in many aspects of daily life where distance may express relationship and cultural norms.[1]

---

[1]This chapter is based on the teachings of the late Alexander Mackendrick, Founding Dean of the School of Film and Video at the California Institute of the Arts. Mr. Mackendrick directed such great films as *The Man in the White Suit, The Ladykillers,* and *The Sweet Smell of Success.* Mackendrick's book, *Film Grammar and Dramatic Form* will be published by Faber & Faber in 2001.

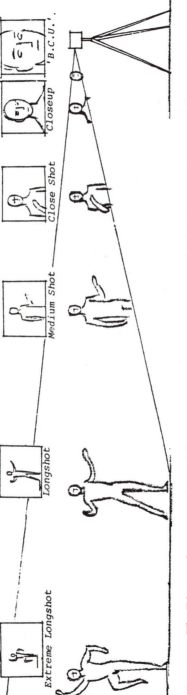

FIGURE 4.1   The Distance between Actor and Camera. Illustration by permission of the Estate of Alexander Mackendrik, 1995.

Distance can be a function of societal class: kings and queens, for instance, neither may be approached too closely, nor may you sit in their presence unless invited. In ordinary life, people who feel the need to maintain an air of authority will often remain at some distance and even force others to take lower positions: the Hollywood stereotype of the agent or executive behind the big desk with the client peering up at them from a low chair is not entirely without foundation.

Proximity also reflects levels of trust. In general, we only let those we trust get close to us. This may partly be a residue of historical circumstances: When men wore swords, for instance, you did not let an enemy get so close that you would be unable to draw. Today, we will often demonstrate trust by coming close and even touching someone. When this is done by strangers or someone we mistrust, it feels like an intrusion.

Distance can also reflect levels of privacy. When we are in a crowd, we can exclude the others by drawing close to one person. On a movie set, for instance, the director will often take one of the actors aside for a private note. Conversely, it is a terrible insult if someone complains or confronts someone "in front of everybody." Even when we are not in a group, we increase intimacy by drawing close. In his study of proximity, Hall found that we use four basic distances, each of which implies a different kind of relationship (see Figure 4.2).

A

B

C

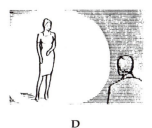

D

FIGURE 4.2   **Four Distances in Real Life.** *A.* **Intimate;** *B.* **Personal;** *C.* **Social;** *D.* **Public. Illustrations by permission of the Estate of Alexander Mackendrick, 1995.**

The greatest proximity is called *intimate distance* (Figure 4.2A). From skin contact to about eighteen inches, there is either positive intimacy such as love or comfort, or negative hostility such as extreme anger (as in getting "in your face"). This is a very *private* distance, and if two people get this close while in a group, they are excluding everyone else.

From eighteen inches to four feet, we enter the *personal distance* (Figure 4.2B). This is still a fairly intimate distance, reserved for friends; strangers who come closer than "arm's length" are threatening or intrusive. This is no longer a private distance, and in a group it implies a special relationship but not an exclusion of the others present.

The *social distance* (Figure 4.2C) is from four to twelve feet and is used for business or casual interaction. This is the most common distance when a group is interacting. Behavior at this distance is not at all private and begins to take on some "public" aspects, so that speech may become more deliberate and words more carefully chosen. Posture and body language communicate as much at this distance as do facial expressions.

When we are more than about twelve feet away, we are in fully *public distance* (Figure 4.2D). Here we are "keeping our distance," and we may slightly exaggerate our gestures and speech in order to "project." The further back we get, the more impersonal we become.

Screen Size and the Actor

The qualities associated with each of the four distances in real life can be applied directly to the equivalent distances between camera and actor, and therefore to the different shot sizes. The film audience is put in the position of the camera as an "unseen observer;" the closer the camera is, the greater our involvement with the character and his or her inner life and the greater the dramatic tension. As the camera moves further away, we become more objective and dramatic tension lessens.

Each shot size alters the behavior required from the actor. The main shot sizes shown in Figure 4.3 give examples of each from the famous "crop dusting scene" in Alfred Hitchcock's *North by Northwest*.

The opening shot of the scene is the greatest distance used in film, the *extreme longshot* (see Figure 4.3A). The shot gives us the empty expanse of farmland, and the hero (played by Cary Grant) can barely be seen. At this distance, the emphasis is on the environment itself; the actor is only an element within it and is so small in the frame that a *photo double* may be used.

The second shot in the scene is slightly closer, a **long shot** (Figure 4.3B). Here Cary Grant's figure is full length but still not recognizable as an individual. This shot emphasizes the relationship between the figure and the environment, stressing Grant's aloneness within the expanse of nothingness around him. This screen size corresponds to Hall's *public distance*. The actor's

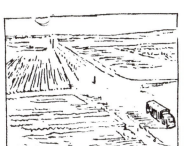

A

B

C

D

E

F

G

FIGURE 4.3 The Seven Screen Sizes. From Alfred Hitchcock's *North by Northwest.* **A. Extreme Longshot;** *B.* **Longshot.** *C.* **Medium Shot;** *D.* **Medium Close Shot;** *E.* **Close Shot;** *F.* **Close-up;** *G.* **Extreme (or Big) Closeup. Illustrations by permission of the Estate of Alexander Mackendrick, 1995.**

performance at this distance will need to be on a scale that would work for a large theater, with slightly exaggerated posture and gestures.

In the third shot of the scene, the camera moves in to a *medium shot* which corresponds to Hall's *social distance* (Figure 4.3C). This is a size for a conversational level of behavior. Because we can see the actor's entire torso, we can read body language well. This is a size in which the actor can use a scale of performance that would serve as good naturalistic acting in a small theater.

A few shots later, we move into a *medium close shot* (Figure 4.3D) that is still in the realm of social distance, but with a slightly stronger emphasis on facial expression. It is just close enough to appreciate feeling and thought in the actor's face, but still far enough to read overall body language as well. This is the most common screen size. The camera is now closer than any theatre audience could ever be, and the actor must provide a rich inner life of thoughts and feelings.

The camera next moves into the area of *personal distance* in what is called a **close shot** (not yet as close as a close-up). This size cuts the actor off at the level of the chest, de-emphasizing body language and throwing primary focus to facial expression (Figure 4.3E). From this distance inward, we get an almost analytical view of the actor's inner world. In the scene from *North by Northwest,* Hitchcock uses this size to register Cary Grant's realization that the cropdusting plane is indeed attacking him.

In the **close-up** (Figure 4.3F), we move into *intimate distance.* Head and shoulders only, the closeup is reserved for moments of strong feeling and important realizations, like the critical moment of Nurse Evers' recognition in the sample scene from *Miss Evers' Boys.* In this size, *subtext* (the actor's inner thought and feeling) becomes easily discernible and speech becomes almost superfluous. The camera is now peering directly *into* the actor's mind, and mental and emotional preparation must be impeccable. The actor's real life scale of behavior may actually be too big here, and he or she may have to suppress their normal expressive behavior. When Sir Laurence Olivier accepted his Oscar for lifetime achievement, he credited a boyhood class in which the students created *tableau vivants* (living pictures), frozen recreations of famous paintings. This experience, he said, taught him the indispensable camera skill of "doing nothing."

In the last example from the scene from *North by Northwest,* Hitchcock's camera zooms rapidly into Grant's face in an *extreme close-up* (**ECU**) (Figure 4.3G). This is a shot that is used sparingly by seasoned directors, who reserve it for only the most deeply felt, complex, or tension-filled moments. Actors are almost never required to speak during a big closeup since this shot expresses thought and feeling that is "beyond words." Here the audience is thrust forcibly into the position of the character and "empathy" is at the maximum. For the actor, the requirements are the same as for a close-up, with an even greater stillness and reliance on inner life.

Notice how Hitchcock purposely began this scene by placing the camera as far away as possible, then gradually worked it closer and closer as dramatic tension built and we became more and more involved with the plight of the hero. Moving in as the scene progresses is an extremely common camera strategy; it reflects the structure of most scenes in which rising tension leads to a crisis (a "turning point,") making it natural for the camera to move closer as the crisis approaches.

Film actors come to sense in advance how a scene is likely to be shot. If you were playing Miss Evers in our sample scene, for example, you would know as soon as you read the scene that your reaction to Douglas' bad news ("autopsy") will most likely be a close-up. Such understanding of the strategy of shooting helps film actors to prepare their performances. Sensing in advance where the dramatic and emotional heart of the scene is, they will lay down a master which provides a firm foundation for the subsequent coverage, adjusting their sense of scale as the camera begins to move in.

As shooting progresses, actors will often ask the DP or camera operator what the size of a shot is; they may ask, "Where are you cutting me?" meaning where on their body is the bottom edge of the frame. (More on this in the next chapter.)

Exercise 4.1: Shot Sizes

A. Shoot your scene four times: once in a full-figure long shot, once in a hip-length medium shot, once in a chest-level close shot, and once in a big close-up. Do you "feel" the proximity of the camera? Are you intuitively adjusting the scale of your performance as the camera comes nearer? Study the results.

B. How would you edit your scene from these shots? If you have the equipment, try a simple assembly edit from these four sources.

Summary

Your first concern about the camera is its proximity. The closer it is, the bigger you are within the frame. The relative distance between actor and camera, then, determines **shot size.** Shot size affects our attitude in the same way that our proximity to others affects us in real life. In everyday life we tend to use four basic distances: intimate, private, social, and public. The qualities associated with each of these four distances in real life can be applied directly to the equivalent distances between camera and actor, and therefore to the different shot sizes. The film audience is put in the position of the camera as an "unseen observer;" the closer the camera is, the greater our involvement with the character and his or her inner life, and the greater the dramatic tension. As the camera moves further away, we become more objective and dramatic tension lessens. Film actors come to sense in advance how a scene is likely to be shot. Such understanding of the strategy of shooting helps film actors to prepare their performances.

5 Teamwork

Filmmaking is the most collaborative of all the arts, and more people with widely varied skills participate actively in the shooting of a film than are involved in the creation of any other kind of artwork. All these people must align their efforts toward the common goal; when they do, it creates an energy that is greater than the sum of its parts, and all are empowered to do their best work.

This kind of teamwork results when three conditions have been met: first, each member of the team must have a strong *commitment* to the common purpose; second, each must *respect* and support the others; third, there must be the possibility of free and open *communication* so that the inevitable problems can be worked out. These conditions make for a truly "happy set."

As an actor, you have a responsibility to contribute to each of these conditions. First, you need commitment on several levels: to your own talent, to each role you play, to each script you perform, to each company of which you are a member, and to the audience you will ultimately serve through your work. Second, you must respect and support the skill of your fellow actors, the director, and every single member of the crew. And finally, you must remain open to others with their opinions and express your own needs with tact and consideration.

Commitment, respect, and communication: these are the cornerstones of teamwork and are equal in importance to all your other acting skills.

Blocking for the Camera

Blocking can be determined by two different methods. In one, the actors are allowed to initiate movement by following their natural impulses; the director and DP then decide how to shoot the resulting blocking. In another, the positions of the actors may be determined entirely by the way the scene is going to be shot. Some few directors, like Alfred Hitchcock, actually prepare "storyboards" which determine the composition of each shot in advance, and the actors are blocked accordingly. Most directors work somewhere between these extremes, collaborating with the actors and the DP to develop the strategy for shooting the scene.

When the director gives movement instructions, he or she will likely use the same terminology used in the live theater. Moving **upstage** is to move away from the camera because stages were at one time sloped away from the audience to enhance the illusion of perspective; for the same reason, moving **downstage** is to come closer to camera. Side-to-side movements are either **stage right or left,** meaning the actor's right or left as they face the camera, or **camera right or left,** meaning right or left from the camera's point of view. Turning *in* means toward the camera; turning *out* means away from the camera.

As the scene is laid out, the various positions of the actors are marked on the floor, a different color of tape being used for each actor. Whenever an actor moves (*make a cross*) to a new position, a new **mark** is made. The sequence of positions are referred to by numbers, and the director may ask the actors to "go to number three." When the scene is going to be restarted from the beginning, the call is to go "back to one."

The marks may be simple lines on the floor when the position is not too critical. Usually, however, the mark will be a "T" and you are expected to end a cross with a foot straddling either side of the "T," toes touching the crossbar (see Figure 5.1). If the position is especially critical, as it may be in extreme close-ups, tight two shots, or over-the-shoulder shots, it may even be necessary for your weight to be on one foot or the other. Of course, all this must be done without looking down and without distraction or self-consciousness. Individual rehearsal is the solution, repeating the move several times until the rhythm and spatial sense of it become automatic.

The camera requires that you move just a little more slowly than normal when you make a cross, and when on your mark you must *stand still.* Indeed, just shifting your weight from foot to foot, or forward and backward, will cause your head to move and drive the camera crew crazy. You may also be going in and out of focus, since the camera's **depth of field** (the range in which you are perfectly in focus) may be only a few inches. In addition, the editor cannot cut from one shot to another if there is motion in either

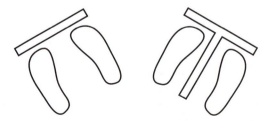

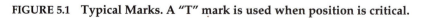

FIGURE 5.1   Typical Marks. A "T" mark is used when position is critical.

unless that motion is perfectly synchronized—which happens only when two cameras are used simultaneously, as they sometimes are. When two cameras are shooting simultaneously, by the way, they are usually on the same angle in two different sizes, such as medium and close. In this case, you perform in a scale appropriate to the closest of the two shots.

As difficult as **hitting your marks** sounds, this critical positioning becomes second nature after a time. By concentrating on your character's action and relating it to the movement required by the blocking, you will naturally make the correct movements to the correct locations.

Exercise 5.1: Blocking

With someone serving as your director and someone else as the DP/camera operator, block your scene, inventing movement if none is otherwise required. Lay down marks at each principal position. Shoot the scene in master. Study the result: Did you hit your marks? Did the marks distract you?

Group Shots

There will be many times when you are literally sharing the lens with your fellow actors. Group shots, such as doubles and triples, make some specific demands on you. Let's use the **two-shot** as our model.

There are three basic forms of the two-shot, as illustrated in Figure 5.2. The first is a *medium two-shot* which shows both figures in relation to each other. When the two actors in a shot are given equal importance, so that neither is favored over the other, the shot is said to be "fifty-fifty."

The second is an *over-the-shoulder (OTS) close-shot* (Figure 5.2B). In the illustration, this shot favors the man and is close enough to show his thought and feeling clearly, while having the girl's shoulder in the frame keeps their relationship important. If the camera were to move in even closer for a single of the man without the girl's shoulder, the emphasis would shift from the relationship to him as an individual. This would be done only if his reaction to something in the scene were a major story point or character development.

The third shot in the illustration is a *complementary two-shot* (Figure 5.2C). It is called "complementary" because it gives an equal but opposite emphasis to the girl. In order to be able to cut smoothly from side to side, the complementary shots must be the same size, and the lens must be at the same angle to the eye-line between the two actors.

You can see in these drawings how each actor is "**cheating** their look" a little toward the camera by looking at the on-camera side of the other actor's face. They are also cheating slightly the distance between them, standing slightly closer in the OTS shots than they were in the master (more about

A   B

C

FIGURE 5.2   Two-Shots from *North by Northwest*. *A*. Medium Two-Shot; *B*. Over-the-Shoulder Close Shot; *C*. Complementary Two-Shot. Illustrations by permission of the Estate of Alexander Mackendrick, 1995.

cheating in the next chapter). And of course, the scale of their performances is appropriate for both the size of the shot and the "personal distance" between them.

In a group shot, there is concern for shadows that the actors may cast on one another. While this is mostly a lighting problem to be solved by the DP, you, the actor, will have to be aware of it and, if necessary, cheat slightly to keep your shadow off your partner's face.

If you are providing the shoulder in an OTS shot, your positioning is extremely critical; the camera operator may actually have to place you by hand. Moving into this kind of shot and hitting that exact placement is very difficult; once there you will have to remain perfectly still, without shifting your weight.

Eye-Lines

When two or more actors are in a shot, their eyes naturally connect, however much they may need to "cheat their looks" toward the camera. When the camera moves in to do a single of one actor or the other, the apparent position of the unseen off-camera character must be correct to maintain the apparent relationship between them.

In practice, the eye-line in a single will be slightly closer to the lens (more "on the lens") than in an OTS shot. In complementary singles, or in singles within group shots, the eye-line of each of the other characters must be carefully established by the camera operator or DP. Again, the eye-lines will be slightly closer to the lens than they were in the actual situation. They will also be closer to one another, since the movement of the actor's eyes in the single will exaggerate the apparent distance between the other characters.

For instance, Figure 5.3A shows the master positions of five actors in a scene in which one actor (A) is standing at the end of a dining room table at which the others are sitting. The camera is at the position indicated. In Figure 5.3B the camera has moved in to cover a single of actor A from a new angle,

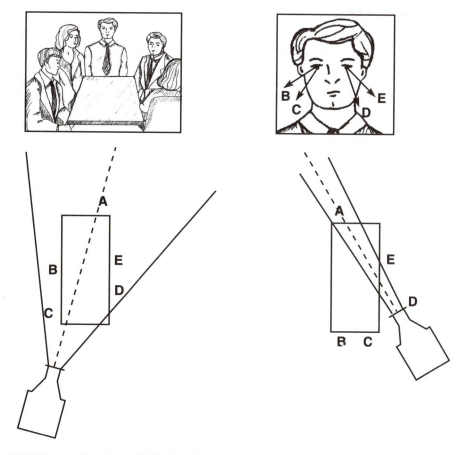

FIGURE 5.3 Blocking Shifted for Eye-Lines. *A*. The Master; *B*. Blocking Shifted for the Single.

and the other actors are placed as shown to provide the correct eye-lines. The new positions are explained by noticing the center line of each shot: in the master, *A* looked toward the left side of the frame when looking at *D* and *E* (that is, his look was "left to right" for them); he looked toward the right side of the frame when he looked at *B* and *C* (his look was "right to left" for them). In the single, the positions of the other actors maintain this same set of looks, but they are all closer to the camera, permitting *A* to play to them without turning away from the lens.

Actors have the responsibility to serve one another by providing off-camera eye-lines and, when doing so, to play the scene with full vigor and good eye contact. This will sometimes require crouching directly next to the camera, as is actor *D* in the illustration. This is done eagerly, since every actor knows that they depend on the others to serve them in the same way.

Exercise 5.2: Two-Shots

Shoot a portion of your scene using the three basic two-shots illustrated in Figure 5.1. For the master, stand about 18 inches away from one another and shoot a fifty-fifty medium two-shot. Then move the camera and shoot complementary OTS shots on each side. Adjust your position and eye-lines as needed. Study the results: Could it be cut together? What adjustments did you have to make?

Overlapping

The problem of "overlapping" refers to a kind of verbal cheating required by the editing process. The sound perspective of each shot is designed to reflect the camera's position, with character's nearer the camera being louder than those farther away. For that reason, when the editor cuts from one shot to another, the sound track usually needs to go along with the cut; that is, the sound from one take cannot usually be used for another. The problem for the editor is to find a moment of silence between words of the dialogue in which to make the cut from one shot to another.

If more than one actor is speaking at a time ("overlapping dialogue"), this moment of silence may not exist. For this reason, actors are usually asked to "cheat" their dialogue by inserting a split-second of silence between speeches. When the scene is edited, this split second can be removed to make the dialogue flow realistically. Since the moment of silence has to exist on "both sides" of the cut, (that is, in every shot made of the scene) overlapping may be prohibited at all times.

No matter how accustomed you may get to delivering your lines in this way, it remains an unnatural way of speaking, and often produces an artificial effect. For this reason, directors who are primarily concerned with the naturalness of the performance tend to allow overlapping. This drives editors to distraction and has the unfortunate effect of requiring a lot of looping (ADR) in which both sides of the scene (that is, the speeches of both actors) may need to be replaced.

Since overlapping is often prohibited, it is a good idea to become comfortable with this manner of delivery. It can be "justified" by slowing down your reaction time so that there is a moment in which you process what you have heard from the other character before you answer.

Exercise 5.3: Overlapping

Perform your scene without overlapping. Try to keep the delay between speeches minimal, but clean. Can you make the delay a "natural" part of your performance?

Summary

Filmmaking is the most collaborative of all the arts. People with widely varied skills must align their efforts toward the common goal; when they do, it creates an energy that is greater than the sum of its parts. This kind of teamwork results when each member of the team must has a strong *commitment* to the common purpose, when each *respects* and supports the others, and when there is free and open *communication.*

When work begins, the blocking for the scene is established with each actor's position marked on the floor. Whenever the actor moves (crosses) to a new position, a new mark is made. A mark will most often be a "T," and you are expected to end a cross with a foot straddling either side of the "T," toes touching the crossbar. This must be done without looking down and without distraction or self-consciousness. The camera requires that you move just a little more slowly than normal when you make a cross, and when on your mark you must *stand still.*

When two or more actors are in a scene, their eye-lines must be correct to maintain the apparent relationship between them. Actors have the responsibility to serve one another by providing off-camera eye-lines and, when doing so, to play the scene with full vigor and good eye contact. When the editor cuts from one shot to another, the sound track usually needs to go along with the cut. This requires a moment of silence between words of the dialogue in which to make the cut. For this reason, actors are usually asked to avoid overlapping their dialogue by inserting a split-second of silence between speeches.

6 Continuity

The piecemeal nature of film shooting makes continuity a major concern on several levels. In the largest sense, the story itself must have continuity. Each scene must flow logically out of the scene before it and lead into the scene to follow, building to the crisis and climax of the entire story. To ensure scene-to-scene continuity in your performance as an actor, you carefully review the scenes preceding and following each scene before you shoot it to be sure it fits into the overall flow and arc of your role.

Besides this scene-to-scene continuity, your performance must also have continuity from master to coverage and from take to take. This is called **matching,** and it is necessary to give the editor free choice of which shots and which takes to select when assembling the scene. No matter how wonderful a performance may be, it is of little use if it won't cut together. There are several ways in which your performance must match: emotional levels, rhythm, timing of business, and position. Let's look at each.

Matching Levels of Intensity

Many film actors instinctively want to "save" their emotional ammunition for the critical moments which they expect will be shot in close-up. You sometimes hear them advise one another, "Don't blow it in the master," or "Save it for the close-up." This, however, is usually a poor strategy. The master shot establishes the baseline that subsequent shots must match. Once the master is shot, the overall dramatic structure of the scene, the relative level of your emotional intensity, and all the visible aspects of your performance must remain sufficiently consistent to permit the editor to cut from one shot to another. This means that the master must lay down a firm foundation for the coverage, and your performance in the master should be as complete and rich as you can make it. Besides, there is no guarantee that the close-ups will necessarily be used (or even shot), so your performance in the master had better be good.

The only exceptions are scenes that require emotional outbursts so extreme that they are draining; in these cases, you probably do need to "save it" for the close-up, and you should discuss this problem with your director. Some directors like to shoot close-ups last because the previous wider shots serve as rehearsal for the actor. Other directors may prefer to capture certain moments early, when they are completely spontaneous. Likewise, some actors get better with repeated takes; others tend to go stale. If you find that you have such a predisposition, you might communicate it to privately to your director.

In actual practice, your coverage will inevitably be slightly different from the master in emotional tone no matter how hard you try to keep it consistent. Your performance may develop greater richness and depth because of sheer repetition and because your director will be working with you to achieve the results needed as the camera moves in. Also, masters are wider than coverage, and it is natural for close-ups to summon greater depth and intensity of thought and feeling. Aside from these subtle emotional differences, however, the mechanics of your performance (your position, the timing of your business, and so on) must match from master to coverage, and from take to take.

Matching Rhythm and Tempo

The basic rhythms and tempos of your performance must also match. The rhythm of the scene is established by the structure of beats and crisis as provided by the writer and interpreted by you and your director (much more about this in Part Two). Because a good editor will cut the scene in a way that reflects this underlying dramatic structure, you cannot radically alter it once the master is shot.

The tempo of the scene must also match fairly well: if a cut is made between takes in which your performance tempo varies too greatly, the result will seem disjointed. Tempo, of course, does not remain perfectly regular throughout a scene; it naturally changes as the action and emotion change, but the timing and degree of these changes should be maintained between master and coverage and from take to take. The exception to this rule occurs when you are instructed to make a change by your director. He or she will know which takes will probably be used and whether a shot that varies from others can be cut into the scene.

Exercise 6.1: Matching Intensity and Rhythm

Shoot a master of your scene, no closer than a medium shot. Then select an important section, especially one which makes a strong emotional demand, and move in for close shots or close-ups. Study the result. Could your coverage be cut into the master? (If you have the necessary equipment, you can make a simple assembly edit.)

Matching Business and Props

There are a number of purely mechanical aspects of your performance which must also match, such as the timing of business to the lines and your positioning. These may in fact be the most bothersome aspects of continuity. Remembering precise details like after which word you drank from the glass and how much liquid was in it, can be very distracting. Luckily, the script supervisor will be there to help remind you about such matters. No matter how good her or his memory and notes may be, however, you must share the responsibility for these details of business and blocking.

There are several things you can do to minimize problems in this area. First, *avoid excessive business:* be highly selective in your use of gesture and activities like eating, smoking, and so on. Best of all, use business only to punctuate the structure of the scene and your inner thought process so that it has a natural place in the rhythm of your performance.

Second, *slow down* just a little and *move a bit less.* On a live theater stage, your physical activity is the main source of visual dynamism in the performance, but in film the movement of the camera and the flow of the editing will supply all the visual dynamism necessary. You needn't move at all unless your action demands it. Further, you are easier to photograph and the details of your performance easier to read if you reduce the range and speed of your physical movements (not so much, of course, as to seem unnatural). When it comes to physical movement for the camera, *less is more.*

Props (from "property") can present their own problems. The props are things which the actors touch and use in some way; the rest of the things on the set are called **dressing.** The props have been carefully selected for your use: in the case of personal items which reflect your character's taste or style, such as rings, watches, or eye glasses, a good **prop master** will offer a number of items from which you and your director may select. When a prop has a special importance in a scene, it is called a **hero prop,** and you may have to give it special treatment—it may, for example, have marks of its own on which you must place it just so.

Usually, the prop master will want to put the props in your hands only moments before the scene is shot in order to protect them from damage. You must make it a point to request important personal props early in order to practice your business with them until it becomes automatic, as it would be for your character. Between takes, the prop people will make sure that all props are returned to their starting positions. Actors are notorious for misplacing or damaging props, and this can cause serious delay. A good prop master will never let you leave the set with a prop. Nevertheless, take it upon yourself to treat your props with respect and return them to the prop people when you leave the set.

Exercise 6.2: Matching Business and Props

Repeat your scene. Involve business and props, even if they must be artificially created for the purpose of this exercise. Rehearse briefly, then shoot the master. Ask someone in your group to act as script supervisor and take careful note of your business and all the physical details of your performance. Using the same section as in the previous exercise, shoot coverage that exactly matches the master in all physical details. Study the results. Were you distracted by the mechanics of the scene?

Matching Take to Take

The number of takes a director will make of a given shot depends on how well the work goes, the director's style of working, and the time available to shoot the scene. Episodic television shows are shot in a matter of five or six days and usually strive to keep takes to a minimum, usually no more than two or three. In this situation, retakes are done only if something is technically wrong with the first, such as "soft" (fuzzy) focus or background noise or actors flubbing lines or missing marks. Rarely are repeated takes done in episodic television to get a better performance. Television movies are usually shot in eighteen to twenty-four days, and the average number of takes increases to four or five. Feature films shoot over a matter of months and may do a great many takes; the great director Stanley Kubrick, a true perfectionist, was known to do over one hundred takes of a single shot.

When performing multiple takes of the same shot, you are faced with the problem of maintaining consistency without sacrificing spontaneity and, at the same time, making the adjustments requested by the director. It can be hard to keep a film moment "alive" take after take, especially if the emotional demand is high. The trick is to divest yourself entirely of any memory of the previous takes and to rediscover the scene anew with whatever adjustments are necessary. Every take has to be the "first." It can help to realize that a take will indeed be new each time: You are not a machine and are incapable of doing exactly the same thing twice, albeit the variation may be very tiny. You need only be alert enough to fully experience the differences.

Exercise 6.3: Repeated Takes

Use the take you selected for coverage within your scene. If possible, ask someone to serve as your director and suggest adjustments in the shot. Shoot at least five takes. Study the result: Did you keep it alive? Did it grow? Was it consistent enough to be useful in editing the scene?

Cheating

Because the camera sees things in its own way, you may sometimes be asked to "cheat." This refers to doing something which is not "natural" but will *look* natural to the camera. There are three main things you must sometimes cheat: *Looks, positions,* and *moves.* Cheating a *look* means adjusting your head so that the camera can better see your eyes. The eyes, as we say, are the windows to the soul, and what you do with your eyes is tremendously important in film. As you learned in the last chapter, for example, when you are standing in a tight two-shot and both of you are equal in the frame (fifty-fifty), the camera will not see your faces well unless you cheat in (toward the lens) slightly. Even when the camera is favoring you, as in an over-the-shoulder shot, your eyes will register better if you look into whichever of your partner's eyes is nearest the camera. (Avoid unnaturally shifting your look back and forth from eye to eye, a cheap trick used in the early days of movies by actors who wanted to appear more "dramatic.")

Cheating your *position* means that when the camera is moved to a new angle, the spatial relationships between the actors must be shifted in order to maintain their apparent relationship in the master, as we discussed in the section on eye-lines in the previous chapter. This will be done for you by the DP or camera operator, of course, but be prepared to find yourself standing in different positions every time the camera moves to a new angle. One of the most important cheats of position is that you must usually stand closer to the other actors than you would in real life. The camera dislikes empty space between people. This problem is greatest in television, which has the narrowest frame and requires that everyone be squeezed to fit. (The proportion of the height to the width of the frame, by the way, is called the **aspect ratio.**)

You may also have to cheat the way you hold certain props in order to keep them clearly in or out of frame, such as raising or lowering a glass you are holding; it is awkward if something straddles the edge of the frame, especially if it moves in and out of view. Certain *movements* also have to be cheated when the camera is trying to follow them. Answering a phone when the camera is following the handset up to your face, for instance, requires that you lift the receiver more slowly than in real life. Getting up out of a chair, or sitting, also requires a little more preparation and shift of weight before the rise or fall to give the camera operator a chance to anticipate your movement and keep you in frame.

Exercise 6.4: Cheating

Using the same piece of coverage, change the angle of the camera and add a piece of business which requires the camera to follow a movement, such as sitting or standing. Cheat your positions as needed to maintain the apparent spatial relationship of the master. Also cheat your look closer to the lens. Finally, cheat your movement so it can be followed by the camera. Study the results.

Summary

The piecemeal nature of film shooting makes *continuity* a major concern. Your performance must have continuity from master to coverage and from take to take in order to ensure that the scene can be cut together by the editor. This is called *matching,* and there are several ways in which your performance must match: emotional levels, rhythms and tempo, timing of business and handling of props, position, and matching repeated takes.

Because the camera sees things in its own way, you may sometimes be asked to "cheat." This refers to doing something which is not "natural" but will look natural to the camera. There are three main things you must sometimes cheat: *Looks, positions,* and *moves.*

CHAPTER

7 Working with Multiple Cameras

There are two kinds of shows commonly shot in the so-called three-camera format: **sitcoms** ("situation comedies") and **soap operas.** These may be shot in either film or video, but in either case the simultaneous use of multiple cameras makes special demands on the actor.

Figure 7.1 shows that the three-camera format was originally designed to produce angles similar to the three basic two-shots in single-camera film: a center master and complementary shots from either side. In the illustration, the center camera is getting the master while the two side cameras have the complementary side angles. In recent years, the number of cameras has been increased to four in order to provide even greater flexibility in shooting, though we still refer to this as a "three-camera" setup. The unique aspect of this format is that all the cameras run simultaneously, and the entire output from each camera is recorded. In this way, the performance can be mastered and covered in the same take, greatly reducing the time needed to complete work.

In actual practice, the four cameras are not at all restricted to the basic shots described in Figure 7.1. The director plans shots in advance, and each camera is given a **shot list:** while one camera is getting the shot planned by the director at a particular moment, the others are setting up for the subsequent shots so that a considerable variety of angles and screen sizes can be achieved. The cameras are constantly adjusting for new shots, and this requires tremendous skill from the teams operating the cameras. In the hands of a seasoned director with a top-notch crew, the four camera set-up can produce a surprising variety of angles and sizes, sometimes approaching the range of single-camera shooting (Figure 7.2).

Film versus Video

Although soap operas are more popular than ever and their stars are handsomely paid, they still must be produced as quickly as possible because they air five days a week. This means that there is no time to process film, so soap

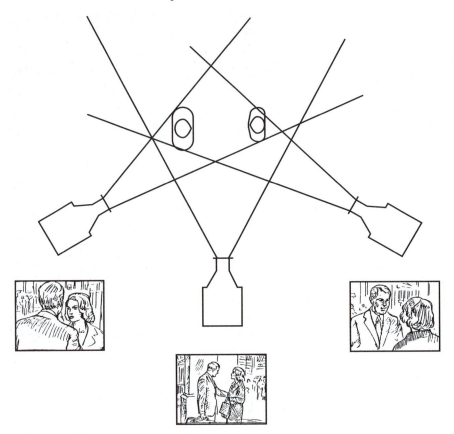

FIGURE 7.1   The Three-Camera Layout.

operas are shot in video. Sitcoms, on the other hand, air only once a week and are usually shot in film to provide better picture quality and a more flexible product for eventual reruns, foreign distribution, and syndication.

There are mechanical differences between video and film. Video cameras are operated by a single person who does all the moving and focusing, with the help of a "cable puller" who manages the umbilical cord which connects the camera to the control board and recorders. Film cameras, on the other hand, even for sitcoms, require the usual three-person crew of operator, focus puller, and dolly grip. Watching four three-person camera crews performing an intricate ballet as they shoot a sitcom can be as much fun as watching the show itself.

In video soap operas, where editing time is extremely limited, the director switches from shot to shot "on the fly" as the scene is performed; only limited changes may later be made. The director sits in a control booth and

FIGURE 7.2   A Sitcom Being Shot. Notice the four cameras and the extra width of the set. Photos courtesy of *Frasier,* **Paramount Studios.**

calls the shots ("ready two, take two") as the **technical director** does the actual switching. The director is also talking constantly to the camera operators to set up and adjust their shots. If the director has to speak to the actors, he or she does so over an intercom or through the **floor manager.**

In film sitcoms, the director needn't call shots and is on the floor with the actors and cameras. He or she is watching what the cameras see via a video assist from each camera displayed on a "quad" monitor and may adjust shots by speaking directly to the camera operators. In general, however, the sitcom director usually pays more attention to the actors' performances than to the cameras and trusts each camera operator to report if they made the shots on their list or not. Meanwhile, a technical director is in a separate booth switching the video assist coming from each film camera from shot to shot; this provides the show watched on monitors by the live audience during the **taping** (although sitcoms are now shot on film, the final performance is still referred to as the "taping").

You can see that in general, the video soap opera director is concentrating mostly on the cameras and only secondarily on the actors, while the reverse is true in filmed sitcoms. As a result, actors in soap operas are a bit more "on their own."

Film and video are under the jurisdictions of two different unions: **AFTRA** (The American Federation of Television and Radio Artists) for video, and **SAG** (The Screen Actors Guild) for film. These two unions have different membership requirements, work rules, and pay scales.

Beyond these differences, however, film and video make basically the same demands on the actor. The real differences for an actor are not between film and video, but rather between single-camera and multiple-camera shows, and between sitcoms and soap operas, regardless of which medium is used. In fact, as high-definition (**Hi-Def**) and digital video technology advances, the distinction between film and video becomes less and less important. Some television movies and even feature films are already shot in high definition video, as were parts of *Star Wars: Episode One*.

Acting for Multiple Cameras

There are a few ways in which performing in three-camera shows, be they soap operas or sitcoms, is much closer to live theater than to single-camera acting. First, because master and coverage are being shot at the same time, scenes in three-camera are played through in their entirety and in sequence, rather than piece by piece and out of sequence as in single-camera film. In three-camera shows, then, actors must fulfill the shape and rhythms of the scene in the same way they would in live theater. Second, because all the cameras are rolling at once, the actors must assume that they are always on camera from at least one angle. They must therefore perform continuously as if in close-up throughout the scene, as they would in a small live theater.

The fact that all the cameras run at once and photograph the action from many angles makes the lighting in multiple-camera shows far more general and less subtle than in single-camera film. This makes the problem of one actor casting a shadow on another more severe. The actors must "find their light" and avoid shadows, just as they would on the live stage.

Beyond these common aspects, however, sitcoms and soap operas make radically different demands on the actor. The main differences spring from their different rehearsal and shooting processes, the differences in the intrinsic nature of the material being performed, and whether a live audience is present or not. Let's examine each.

Sitcoms

Performing in a sitcom is very close to acting in a fairly broad comedy in the live theater. The similarity starts with the fact that an audience is present. Ever since Desi Arnaz got the idea of bringing a live audience into the tapings of *I Love Lucy*, a live audience has become essential to the energy and "presence" of sitcom performances. The broad, sometimes farcical, comedic style required for a sitcom flourishes when the actors receive the rush of adrenaline that only a live audience can provide. Moreover, the timing required for good comic delivery, with the set-up and payoff of "three jokes to the page," can be perfected best when the actors are getting the reactions of a live audience. Even though the sitcom audience's presence behind the cameras is important, however, *the actors still play for the cameras* as far as the scope of their movement and vocal projection is concerned.

The rehearsal and shooting process of a sitcom is very similar to live theater. Only one half-hour show is shot per week, so the amount of rehearsal per minute of performance is actually about the same as in an average commercial theater production. Having four or five days of rehearsal allows the actors and the writers to develop the material and the performance in a way that would be impossible in soap operas or in single-camera film. Here, for example, is a typical week on a show like *Frasier, Cheers,* or *Becker;* work on each episode begins on a Wednesday and culminates with the taping the following Tuesday night.

Wednesday: Table reading. The cast meets for a few hours to sit at a large table and read the new script. At the readings and all subsequent rehearsals, the director, producers, and writers provide exuberant laughter; this sometimes seems artificial to an outsider, but it is essential to the actors in developing their comedic timing.

Some of the writers are also producers, and they stay with the show all season long; this provides story and character continuity and makes developmental arcs for the characters possible. Additional writers are brought in to work on specific episodes; in all, the average number of writers is around six.

After the reading, the director and the actors share their ideas with the writers, and, after some discussion, the writers cloister themselves in *the room* to work on improvements. The room is a literal place that is strictly off limits to anyone but the writers, and they sometimes will work through the night to prepare the script for the next day. In fact, the week-long rehearsal period for a sitcom is more for the sake of developing the material than it is for preparing the actors and cameras: they could probably do a show in two days if they had to.

Thursday: Second reading. Again, a table reading is held to test the improvements in the script. After more discussion of the script, the show is put into the set for basic blocking and the development of comic business and "sight gags."

The "standing" or "home" set is familiar to the actors; each character has established their territory and habitual traffic pattern, so the blocking is more or less automatic. The set is laid out as a very wide proscenium set might be arranged in the theater. It is much wider than it will look on camera. The extra width permits the bulky film cameras to move more easily and to get more oblique angles which provide better shot composition. Home sets often contain more than one room; the *Cheers* set included the bar, the office, and the back room. These rooms are side by side, with the adjoining walls swinging so that parts of the set may be opened or closed as needed. If any given episode requires additional sets, they are placed at one end of the stage or the other. Again, after rehearsal, the writers move back to the room.

Friday: Blocking and more rehearsal on the set. The actors get their marks, just as in single-camera film. Positioning is fairly critical since two or more shots from different angles may depend on the actor's placement; but because of more general lighting and greater depth-of-field, the cameras can adjust slightly if an actor is not exactly on the mark.

At this rehearsal, props, special set dressing, and wardrobe are introduced. The director, DP, and first AD are planning the shots. The most recent script improvements from the writers are distributed, and the actors are beginning to commit to their lines.

The Weekend: The writers are probably working over the weekend to improve the script further. Each cast member has a fax machine at home to receive any new pages. If necessary, other writers may be brought in to "punch up" the script; these are specialists, sometimes called "body and fender people," who have a knack for recognizing incipient jokes and bringing them into focus.

Occasionally, an outdoor scene or a scene requiring some sort of special effect may be shot separately during the week and inserted into the show at the taping.

Monday: Camera blocking is done today as the full crew reports for the first time (some of these crews work on other shows on other days). The actors may have to assimilate extensive improvements made by the writers over the weekend, and they finally begin to learn their lines in earnest. This is usually a critical day in the development of the show, and energy is high.

Tuesday: Dress rehearsal is held in the afternoon with an invited audience. The large number of **extras** are worked into the show by the second assistant director. Many of these extras have been with the show for some time, and the whole affair has the quality of a party. The dress rehearsal is filmed, and on rare occasions material from it may be used in the broadcast version. After the dress rehearsal, a dinner is served to cast and crew (the principals have a quiet private dinner of their own) as the audience begins to arrive. Improvements from the writers are coming in until the last minute, even between the dress rehearsal and the performance. At "half hour," the actors report to wardrobe, hair, and makeup.

The taping at 7 P.M. that evening has the feeling of an opening night in the theater. A live band is playing and a **"warm-up person,"** a stand-up comedian with considerable familiarity with the show, keeps the audience entertained both before and during breaks in the taping. The audience sits in bleachers across the entire width of the sound stage, so not everyone can see the action when it is on one of the side sets. Most of the time the bulky film cameras make it difficult to see the actors anyway. It matters little, though, because monitors are hung above the audience so everyone can watch a rough version of the show, switched from shot to shot. This is important because the audience's reactions are recorded and serve as the "laugh track" for the show. If a scene has been pre-shot, it will be inserted into the show at the proper point so that the audience's reaction to it can be recorded as well.

As the taping begins, the cast is introduced to the studio audience with much applause. Energy is way up. The floor in front of the set is filled with people: the director, producers, writers, studio and network executives. When actors look toward the audience, they see a virtual mob of people and cameras watching them. During performance, this crowd of cameras and others is in constant motion, and this presents a real test of the actor's concentration (see Figure 7.3).

FIGURE 7.3   What a Sitcom Actor Sees. Besides the four cameras, there is a host of producers, writers, network and studio executives; the audience can be seen in the bleachers in the background. Photo courtesy of *Frasier*, Paramount Studios.

A bell signals the beginning of each take. If during the taping a mistake is made (which is common), the director stops and restarts the show as necessary, usually picking up from some point. Sometimes a scene may be entirely redone.

When a scene is successfully completed, the actors retreat for any necessary costume changes while the sets and cameras are moved into place for the next scene. The warm-up person keeps the audience occupied: the great fear, of course, is that the spectators will grow tired during the four or more hours it will take to tape the show, and their reactions may fall off toward the end. (When necessary, laughter may be "sweetened" by mixing tracks from the afternoon rehearsal into the evening performance, or even by electronic augmentation.)

To avoid exhausting the audience, many of the shots that need to be redone are saved and done as pick-ups after the audience has left. These pick-ups may go on for hours; lines may even be rewritten at this point. I once saw an entirely new ending for an episode of *Cheers* written and shot at two o'clock in the morning.

The next day (Wednesday), the process begins all over again with a table reading of the script for the next episode. Most sitcoms work three consecutive weeks, then take a week off, producing twenty-four or twenty-six shows a season.

Soap Operas

As we have said, "soaps" and sitcoms have some similarities with live theater and with each other: in both, scenes are shot in sequence and in their entirety, stopping and restarting only as necessary; also, the actors in both perform continuously since they are always potentially on camera. But there the similarities end.

Because "soaps" air every weekday, there is little time for rehearsal or for much stopping and starting during the taping. At the end of each day, the scripts for the next day's shooting are distributed, and lines must be learned overnight. The next day, of course, there will probably be rewrites handed out, sometimes just before a scene is shot. Add to this the pressure to complete every scene in one take, and you can see why soap opera actors must have both excellent memories and an almost improvisational skill for thinking on their feet; repeated mistakes are not tolerated.

The nature of the material in soap operas is 180 degrees opposite to sitcoms. Where the sitcom is fast and broad, the soap opera is slow and intensely internal. As a soap opera actor, you have to maintain a very high inner dynamic and emotional level. The inner preparation you will learn in Part Two is of primary importance, along with the ability to personalize and to find great personal importance in the character's needs and circumstances.

Even though viewers become engrossed in the plot of soap operas, the writing is actually character-centered. Viewers care about what is happening *because* they know the characters intimately and identify with them. By living through the internal process of the character fully and with great intensity, the soap opera actor maximizes the audience's opportunity to identify, even with characters who may be unsympathetic in many ways.

Summary

There are two kinds of shows commonly shot in the so-called three-camera format: sitcoms and soap operas. In this format all three cameras run simultaneously so that the performance can be mastered and covered in the same take. Soap operas are shot in video, while sitcoms are usually shot in film. Video cameras are operated by a single person who does all the moving and focusing, while film cameras always require a three-person crew. Film and video make basically the same demands on the actor.

There are a few ways in which performing in three-camera shows, be they soap operas or sitcoms, is closer to live theater than to single-camera acting. First, scenes in three-camera are played through in their entirety and in sequence. Second, actors must perform continuously as if in close-up, as they would in a small live theater. Three-camera actors must also "find their light" and avoid shadows, just as they would on the live stage.

Performing in a sitcom is very close to acting in a fairly broad comedy in the live theater. The similarity starts with the fact that a live audience has become essential to the energy and "presence" of sitcom performances. Even though the sitcom audience's presence behind the cameras is important, the actors still play for the cameras as far as the scope of their movement and vocal projection is concerned. Since only one half-hour episode is shot per week, the amount of sitcom rehearsal allows the material and performance to be developed in a way that would be impossible in soap operas or in single-camera film.

Because "soaps" air every weekday, there is little time for rehearsal or for much stopping and starting during the taping. The soap opera actor has to maintain a very high inner dynamic and emotional level. The inner preparation discussed in Part Two is of primary importance, along with the ability to personalize and to find great personal importance in the character's needs and circumstances.

Preparing Yourself and Your Role

8 The Inner Discipline of Camera Acting

In Part One, you learned a number of the physical conditions which affect the actor's work for the camera. In Part Two, you will explore the way in which the film actor must create a rich, specific, and productive inner world for his or her character. As we said in Part One, our approach is based upon the acting system developed by the great Russian director and teacher Konstantin Stanislavsky. Dissatisfied with the bravura acting style of his time, he created a new system of acting designed to produce greater psychological truthfulness and economy.

Transformation and "the Magic If"

The actor's most fundamental skill is *role-playing,* and it is at work in real life. You play a role every time you enter a social situation and pursue your needs by behaving in certain ways, saying certain things in certain ways to other people, and reacting to the things they do and say to you. It is this adjustment of your behavior to fit your circumstances and those with whom you interact that shapes and expresses your personality, your *character* in everyday life. In fact, you play several roles every day—student, son or daughter, friend, employee—each with its own appropriate behavior, speech, thought and feelings: your own little repertory company.

This is an ongoing process: as your circumstances, needs, and relationships change, they cause changes in you as a person. If you are in a circumstance that forces you to behave in a certain way, and you allow yourself to remain in that situation for a period of time, you start to become the kind of person appropriate to that situation.

This fact was noticed many years ago by the psychologist William James, who said that our personalities are actually composed of many roles. He called these roles our various *me's.* Behind the "me's," he said, there is one consciousness, which he called our *I.* Our "I" is not rigid and is expressed through all of our "me's," even though some of them may be quite different from one another. We may even experience situations in which two or more of our "me's" come into conflict with one another. If you're busy being "buddy" with your friends, or "lover" with that special other, the arrival of parents or a boss may cause an uncomfortable conflict between your roles as "buddy" or "lover" and your roles as "child" or "employee."

Exercise 8.1: Role-Playing in Life

Think about your own experience over the past few days. What roles did you play? How did your situation influence your behavior and feelings? Were there times when you had to switch roles rapidly, or your roles came into conflict?

As you think about the various roles you play in your life, you will notice that your sense of "I" tends to flow into whichever "me" you are being at the moment. Some of your "me's" may be more or less familiar than others, but they are all versions of yourself.

One of your most important skills as a film actor will be *to allow your "I" to flow fully and freely into the new "me" of the role and its world.* You do this not to "be yourself," but to develop a *new version* of yourself. Although quite different from your everyday self, this new version is nevertheless "natural" to you, truthful to the character as created by the writer, and appropriate to the artistic purpose for which the role was created.

Stanislavsky called this process *"the Magic If." If* you live in the world of the character, and *if* you need what the character needs, and *if* you do the things the character does in order to try to satisfy those needs, you naturally, "magically," find your thought, feelings, and behavior changing into that new version of yourself that will be your special way of playing the role.

This ability to become a fictitious character, to completely believe in "the Magic If" and enter a make-believe world and character, is something we all had naturally as children. It is this childlike ability for make-believe that we need to rediscover as film actors, however much we empower it through our adult sense of purpose and technique.

Exercise 8.2: Character in Life

For the next few days, observe your own behavior and those around you. Notice the way you present yourself differently in various circumstances.

1. Notice changes in your physical behavior.
2. Notice changes in your voice, manner of speaking, and choice of words.
3. Notice your choice of clothing and the "props" you use.
4. Notice changes in the way you think and feel.
5. Most of all, notice how you naturally tend to "become" each of the roles you are playing.

Action and Public Solitude

The fully personal inner reality required of the film actor gives special importance to two of the fundamental principles of Stanislavsky's system: *action*
and *public solitude*. He discovered these related principles when he was himself a student actor. Like many young actors, Stanislavsky suffered from stage
fright; he became tense and distracted on stage because he was aware of
being watched. One day, his teacher gave him a simple task: he was to go up
onto the stage and count the floorboards while the class went on with other
business. Stanislavsky dutifully followed these seemingly inane instructions
and was soon busy counting the floorboards, totally engrossed in his task.
Suddenly he looked up and found the class watching him; for the first time
he had been on stage without self-consciousness. The experience was liberating
and exhilarating.

Stanislavsky realized that it was his total focus on his task that had
allowed him to forget about being watched. From this experience, he developed the idea of giving the character an objective in each moment of the performance; this objective, he reasoned, would serve the actor as a "dramatic
task" that, like counting the floorboards, would provide a point of concentration that could eliminate or at least reduce self-consciousness. He called
the actor's total commitment to the character's objective being *in action*, and
the unselfconscious state it produced *public solitude*. Behavior produced in true
public solitude is uncontaminated by the actor's self-awareness and has the
integrity and authenticity required by the camera. This is why the basic concepts of the Stanislavsky approach have become the foundation of film acting,
and most of our greatest film actors have been trained in this way. We will
go on to examine these concepts in detail in the following chapters.

Justification

Another fundamental principle of the Stanislavsky system is designed to
ensure economy of performance by avoiding meaningless activity. It states
that everything the actor does as the character must be *justified* by growing
directly out of the needs of the character. As he put it:

> There are no physical actions divorced from some desire, some effort in some
> direction, some objective . . . Everything that happens on the stage has a definite
> purpose.[1]

Specifically, Stanislavsky taught that the character's needs and desires cause
them to do something (their *action*) in an effort to achieve a desired goal (their

[1]Stanislavsky, *An Actor's Handbook*, p. 8.

objective, though the terms "intention" or "task" are sometimes used to mean the same thing). In short, *need causes action directed toward an objective.* The more you engross yourself in this process and surrender yourself to your character's needs, actions, and objectives, the more in action you are, and with action comes public solitude and transformation.

You have seen people in real life in action and in public solitude: an athlete executing a difficult play, people arguing a deeply felt issue, a student studying for a big test, lovers absorbed in each other. All these people have a personally significant objective, and as a result they are totally focused on what they are doing. The more important their objective, the more complete their focus, and the more unself-conscious and committed they become. Just so, public solitude achieved through total commitment to an objective is how the film actor can best produce the authentic and complete reality demanded by the camera. (This is why most film actors don't want to watch dailies during shooting—it interferes with their involvement in the inner life of the character and encourages self-awareness. Some find watching themselves on screen uncomfortable even after the film is completed.)

You have been in action many times in your life and therefore in public solitude. Think back to those experiences in which you were totally "tuned in" to what you were doing, so engrossed in your activity that you became totally unself-conscious, oblivious to passing time or to outside distractions. The state of mind you discovered during these experiences can be a foundation for your work in front of the camera.

Exercise 8.3: Action in Life

A. For the next few days, notice people who are in action: What are they doing? How do they seem to feel about it? What makes them interesting? Imagine how you might capture such moments on film.

B. Think about those times when you have been in action yourself. Select one such time and relive it in your imagination. Relax and enter into the fantasy fully. Consider what made it possible for you to achieve this level of complete commitment and focus: What personal needs were motivating you? What feelings, ideas, or beliefs were at work? How did your circumstances effect you? What specifically did you want? What did you do to try to get it?

In the following chapters, we will examine the specifics of action and how it can help you enter into the life of your character and thereby help you to create performances with the kind of integrity that will stand up to the scrutiny of the camera.

Indicating

Nothing stands in the way of true transformation more often than an actor's attempt to show the audience what their character is feeling and thinking. Such "illustrative" acting falsifies the character's reality. We call it *indicating*; you are indicating whenever you are *showing* instead of simply *doing*.

Actors indicate for various reasons: because it is a way of maintaining control over the performance; because it "feels" like some mistaken notion of acting; but most often because it is a way of trying to earn the audience's approval. Instead of simply doing what their character is doing, they are also trying to show us how the character feels, or what kind of a character they are. Their performance is saying "Hey, look at how angry I am," or "Look at what a victim I am." Because indicating contaminates the character's reality with elements of the actor's awareness, it always feels unbelievable and never more so than in front of a camera.

Our sense of whether someone is believable, on screen or in life, is based on the fact that role-playing behavior always sends two kinds of messages: one is the impression we are consciously trying to make, the other is the unconscious behavior that reveals what we really believe and feel. In every-day life we intuitively read unconscious behavior, such as "body language" and tell-tale qualities of the voice, and compare these unconscious expressions with the conscious message being delivered. When the two are consistent, we judge the person to be believable; when they are inconsistent, we feel that the person is insincere. For example, if I am trying to convince you that I am extremely interested in what you are saying, but you catch me fidgeting, you reject my performance. The screen audience's scrutiny of unconscious behavior, magnified by the acuteness of the camera, is even more rigorous. For this reason, the film actor must achieve a complete unity of conscious and unconscious behavior; we say that he or she cannot be "acting" at all.

If you can learn to recognize indicating and avoid it by committing to a specific action, you will find that you will automatically express all the emotion and sense of character needed. Your job is not to *show* the camera anything, it is simply to *do* what your character does as completely and accurately as you can. Remember, you are not performing *for* the camera, you are creating real behavior that the camera only "happens" to see. You must trust your director and the camera team to capture your performance; you need not hand it to them on a plate.

Exercise 8.4: A Simple Task

Invent a character in a dramatic situation: a condemned man waiting for the governor to call, a bride apprehensively waiting to walk down the aisle. Next, select a simple physical activity that such a person might be doing: playing solitaire or arranging the flowers in the bridal bouquet. Record yourself performing this task. Watch the results: Compare what you see with your own sense of being in action. Were you indicating? How strong is your impulse to "show" instead of "do"?

Transformation for the Camera

If you allow "the Magic If" to operate by surrendering fully to your character's world, needs, actions, and objectives, avoiding the pitfall of indicating, you will undergo transformation as a new "me" emerges. This also can happen before a live audience, of course, but as we have said, the camera imposes a more severe test of the completeness of the transformation. It also imposes certain limitations on it.

The stage permits transformation on a physical as well as a psychological level, but the camera has little tolerance for physical transformation; even extensive and elaborate makeup tricks will fail to persuade unless the actor's inner reality has been brought into complete harmony with the character's external appearance. Transformation for the camera must be of a much more subtle and psychological kind. For this reason, there is a wider range of characters that an actor may play on the stage than on the screen.

This inner reality is why you will be cast in film and television roles that are very close to your physical appearance and to your personality type. This is not as limiting as it may sound; remember that you have a vast personal potential for all sorts of "me's." Film acting will give you a chance to explore that potential. Think of film acting, then, not so much self-*expression* as self-*expansion*. This expansion, this exploration of new forms of the self, is the most exciting aspect of the film actor's creative process. Film acting is a matter not of seeming or being, but of one of *becoming,* of finding and unfolding entirely new inner worlds. This is an exciting challenge demanding a high level of personal courage, curiosity, and transformational skill.

In short, the rigor imposed by the camera makes film acting more a *spiritual* than a technical discipline.

Summary

The actor's most fundamental skill is *role-playing.* You play a role every time you enter a social situation and pursue your needs by behaving in certain ways. William James said that our personalities are actually composed of many roles, which he called our various *me's.* Behind the "me's," he said, there is one consciousness, which he called our *I.* One of your most important skills as a film actor will be *to allow your "I" to flow fully and freely into the new "me" of the role and its world.* You do this not to "be yourself," but to develop a *new version* of yourself which is nevertheless "natural" to you. Stanislavsky called this process *"the Magic If."* If you live in the world of the character, and *if* you need what the character needs, and *if* you do the things the character does in order to try to satisfy those needs, you naturally, "magically," find your thought, feelings, and behavior changing into that new version of yourself that will be your special way of playing the role.

Stanislavsky called the actor's total commitment to the character's objective being *in action,* and the unselfconscious state it produced *public solitude.* A related principle is that everything the actor does as the character must be *justified* by growing directly out of the needs of the character. In short, *need causes action directed toward an objective.*

Nothing stands in the way of true transformation more often than an actor's attempt to show the audience what their character is feeling and thinking. Such "illustrative" acting falsifies the character's reality. We call it *indicating;* you are indicating whenever you are *showing* instead of simply *doing.*

Because the camera has little tolerance for physical transformation, there is a wider range of characters that an actor may play on the stage than on the screen. This is not as limiting as it may sound; you have a vast personal potential for all sorts of "me's." Film acting will give you a chance to explore that potential. Think of film acting, then, not so much self-*expression* as self-*expansion.* In short, the rigor imposed by the camera makes film acting more a *spiritual* than a technical discipline.

9

Inner Action

A novelist can take you inside a character's mind to reveal the inner process of thought that lies beneath their behavior, but a screenwriter can only imply it through the character's language and actions. As an actor, you will learn to understand the psychology of action so that you can recreate for yourself the inner world beneath the surface of the script. This will be the greatest creative and personal contribution you will make to your performance, and it will be the foundation of all the other work you do.

Let's examine the psychology of action by setting up a hypothetical situation. Imagine that you see a casting notice for a film I am directing, and it lists a part that would be perfect for you. Here's what happens, step-by-step: First, you see the notice; we will call this your *stimulus*. The stimulus arouses both your desire to play the part and your fear of rejection; we will call this mixture of anticipation and anxiety your *attitude*. Like most actors, your desire for success outweighs your fear of failure, so you begin to *consider* various strategies for winning the part; you consider how best to present yourself at the audition, what you might wear, how to approach the role, and so on. You then make a *choice* of the strategy that seems to have the best chance of success in the given circumstances. Finally, you commit to the course of *action* you have chosen and audition.

This whole sequence is the mental process by which a purposeful action is formed: *a stimulus arouses an attitude, alternatives are considered, and a strategic choice is made that results in action directed toward an objective.*

You can see this process represented graphically in Figure 9.1. The large circle represents your skin, the boundary between your "outer" and "inner" worlds. The *stimulus* enters you through seeing or hearing. Once inside you, it arouses a particular emotional quality that is your *attitude* toward it.

Your reaction can next take two forms. Some things cause you to have an *automatic* response in which your reaction is immediate and involuntary, bypassing conscious thought (more on this later). On the other hand, you may

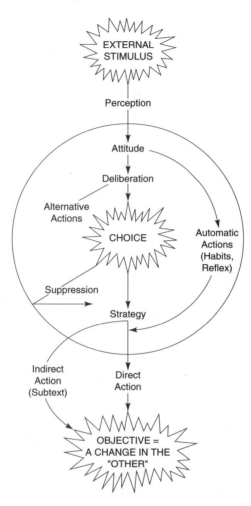

FIGURE 9.1 The Process of Action.

think about it by considering your alternatives. Finally you make a *strategic choice* about how best to proceed.

This choice is at the center of the process: before your choice, you have been reacting to your stimulus, but now your reaction turns into an action directed outward toward your objective. In other words, the inner process of action has two phases: first, an *inward* flow of reaction leading to a choice, followed by an *outward* flow of action directed toward an objective. This explains the old saying that "acting is reacting."

As a film actor, it is this inner process of action that will be the focus of your preparation. The external behavior that results from this process will be allowed to happen in a spontaneous and unpremeditated way when the director calls "action." In this way, the camera will be both intrigued by the richness and specificity of your inner thought process and satisfied by the spontaneity and authenticity of your resultant external behavior.

Seeing and Listening

Actors sometimes fail to react truthfully. They only pretend to receive what is said or done to them, preferring instead the safety of reacting to their own idea of what the other actor says or does. They refuse to make themselves vulnerable by being truly affected by the actions of others. This is a failure that the film actor cannot afford. The camera will see instantly if you attempt to fake or manipulate a reaction.

Nor can the film actor afford to be self-stimulating. You must always react to something "out there" in the scene, something that someone else says or does. Even when a stimulus triggers some important and long-standing need in your character, you cannot play the pre-existent need, only the immediate stimulus. Action lives only in the immediate present and is always directed toward the immediate future. If you allow your awareness to be drawn into the past, you become *reflective* instead of *dramatic*. Although reflection at rare times may be required, it must always be transformed into an action directed toward an immediate objective.

For example, there is a scene in *A Streetcar Named Desire* in which Blanche tells Mitch what happened years ago on the night that her young fiancé killed himself. Too often, actresses play this scene as if the pain in Blanche is the main reason for telling the story. Played in this way, Mitch fades into the background, and the story becomes a monologue instead of a scene. The actress must find the motivation for the story not in her own need but "out there" in Mitch; it is his capacity for understanding that triggers her tremendous need to share, in the hope that he will understand and love her. Her objective is not to relive her pain but to inspire compassion in Mitch.

Remember, then, to react to things that are immediate and external. Film acting is not so much *doing* things as it is allowing yourself to be *made* to do them. Don't let your fear of losing control turn you into a hermetically sealed, self-stimulating actor. Open yourself to what is really happening. Remember, *acting is reacting*.

Exercise 9.1: Reacting

A. Stand in front of the camera. Members of your group are to provide random stimuli: statements, noises, whatever. Record your reactions in a *medium close shot*. Watch the tape to study the quality of your unpremeditated reactions.

B. You and your scene partner sit in chairs and read your scene aloud. Record the reading in a medium shot. Watch the tape to study your reactions to each other: Were you truly listening and reacting or merely giving false, premeditated reactions?

Attitude

When you hear or see something that is significant enough you form an attitude toward it. It may be a threat, a good thing, an opportunity which touches on some need, and so on. Becoming clear about your character's attitude toward each thing that happens to him or her, and allowing those attitudes to become your own, is an important way of entering into the character's way of seeing the world. You may notice that your character has a typical way of reacting to most things; this pattern of reaction expresses the character's attitude toward the world in general. Are they optimistic or pessimistic? Does their attitude reveal any feeling that they have about themselves? Willy Loman in *Death of a Salesman,* for example, is quick to sense any criticism from others; this almost paranoid defensiveness reveals his fundamental insecurity and low self-esteem.

Exercise 9.2: Attitude

A. Answer these questions about your scene:

1. In each of your character's reactions, identify the external and immediate stimulus to which you are responding.
2. Consider what each stimulus means to them; what is their attitude toward each? Does it trigger any needs already within the character?
3. Does your character respond more to some stimuli than to others? How do these sensitivities reflect his or her needs, values, personality, and attitude toward the world and themselves?

B. Based on this study, perform your scene again for the camera. Watch the results: Are you allowing your character's attitude to each stimulus to form naturally, or are you indicating it?

Choice

Because choice is the moment at which reaction turns into action, it is the essence of drama. The most suspenseful moments occur when a character confronts a significant choice; we wonder "what is he or she going to do now?"

The suspense is heightened when the choice is difficult, when the character is choosing between equally compelling (or equally unattractive) alternatives. In tragedy, these choices usually take the form of a "double bind" in which there are no "good" alternatives. In *Miss Evers' Boys,* for example, Nurse Evers is forced to choose between continuing in a program that withholds penicillin from her patients, or leaving them with no treatment or care whatsoever. Her difficult moral choice is the heart of the entire film.

In comedy, on the other hand, the choices are not so serious. In the sample scene from *Cheers,* for example, Carla is faced with the choice of marrying Ludlow or not, but the consequences of either choice are basically good, and as it happens, she gets the best of both worlds.

Choice is the most revealing point in the process of action. In the making of significant choices, your character is responding to needs, to a way of seeing the world, and to relationships, beliefs, and values. If you can identify the factors influencing your character's most significant choices, you will be in touch with everything needed to create the psychological aspect of your characterization. Perhaps more important, living through your character's significant choices is the main mechanism by which "the Magic If" produces transformation. You enter into your character's circumstances as if they are your own and feel their needs as if they are your own. You then make the choices they make and feel those choices as your own. From this process, action will follow naturally and with it will come transformation.

Choice cannot be fully experienced without real alternatives. Unless you have alternatives to consider, you can only "act out" your character's choice, not truly live it out for yourself. In other words, you must consider not only what your character *does,* but also what he or she chooses *not* to do. When your character is presented with a significant choice, you must find for yourself the various alternatives they might consider but reject. The creation of these alternatives is a powerful way for you to enter into your character's mind because they represent an inventory of the way your character sees the world.

Following is a list of all the factors that may influence any particular choice. They may be either internal (in the character's mind), or external (in the character's world).

1. Internal factors influencing choice:
   a. Social background;
   b. Needs and desires;
   c. Psychological processes or "ways of thinking";
   d. Ethical values;
   e. Attitudes toward other characters.
2. External factors influencing choice:
   a. Relationships with other characters;
   b. Social environment;
   c. Physical environment;
   d. Specific immediate circumstances.

Exercise 9.3: Choice

Decide which is the one most significant choice made in this scene by your character. Examine it in detail: What factors influence this choice? Provide alternatives and courses of action your character considers but rejects. Record your scene again with this awareness; take the time to experience the choice fully. Examine the results: Does the choice feel real? Is a sense of character beginning to emerge?

Summary

A purposeful action is formed when *a stimulus arouses an attitude, alternatives are considered, and a strategic choice is made that results in action directed toward an objective.* Some things elicit an *automatic* response in which your reaction is immediate and involuntary; others require you to think about alternatives and to then make a *strategic choice* about how best to proceed. The inner process of action, then, has two phases: first, an *inward* flow of reaction leading to a choice, followed by an *outward* flow of action directed toward an objective. This explains the old saying that "acting is reacting." It is this inner process of action that will be the focus of the film actor's preparation. The external behavior that results will be allowed to happen in a spontaneous and unpremeditated way when the director calls "action."

Action lives only in the immediate present and is always directed toward the immediate future. If you allow your awareness to be drawn into the past, you become *reflective* instead of *dramatic*; though reflection at rare times may be required, it must always be transformed into an action directed toward an immediate objective. Because choice is the moment at which reaction turns into action, it is the essence of drama. In making significant choices, your character is responding to needs, to a way of seeing the world, and to relationships, beliefs, and values. If you can identify the factors influencing your character's most significant choices, you will be in touch with everything needed to create the psychological aspect of your characterization. Perhaps more important, living through your character's significant choices is the main mechanism by which "the Magic If" produces transformation.

CHAPTER

10 Actions and Objectives

A baseball batter rehearses his stance, grip, swing, and breathing; he studies the opposing pitchers; at the plate, he takes note of the wind and the position of the fielders. As he begins to swing at a pitch, however, he ceases to think about all this and focuses his total awareness on the ball. This single objective channels all his energy into his action, the swing. Having this single objective allows the batter to synthesize all his other concerns and all his rehearsed and intuitive skills into a single complete action of mind and body.

For you as an actor, the "ball" is your character's objective, what he or she is trying to accomplish at any given moment. Your focus on this single objective at the moment of action will provide you with the same kind of integration achieved by the baseball batter. It will energize your action and give it power, intensity, and control.

Defining Productive Objectives

When you begin working on a scene, one of your earliest steps is to discover your character's needs and each of the objectives the character pursues to try to satisfy those needs, step-by-step through the scene. You define these objectives in a way which makes them personally important to you, giving you the kind of focus on your dramatic task that the batter has on the ball, thereby producing public solitude. When an objective does both these things—compels your attention and energizes you in a personal way—it is what Stanislavsky called a *productive objective*. Experience has proven that objectives become more productive when they are directed toward a *single, immediate,* and *personally important* goal. Let's examine each.

First, an objective needs to be *singular* because you wish to focus your energy on one thing rather than diffuse it by trying to do two things at once. Imagine a batter trying to hit two balls simultaneously.

Second, the most useful objective is in the *immediate present,* something that can happen right now. The scene must move forward, and your energy must help propel it; never define your character's objective in a way that moves your awareness into yourself or into the past. While the character's needs may be rooted in the past, their action is always directed toward an objective in the immediate present or future.

Finally, an objective must be *personally important* to you, the actor, so that it will engage as much of your own feeling, belief, thought, and unconscious behavior as possible. We can remember these three requirements as the acronym **SIP:** Singular, Immediate, and Personal.

A productive objective will also connect you to the other characters in the scene. The most productive way to define an objective is as *a change you want to bring about in the other character*. One acting teacher even taught his students to think of this as a change in the other character's eyes. If, as Willy Loman, your immediate objective is to get Howard's attention away from the recorder, you can think of wanting "to get him to look at me with interest." This encourages you to play into your partner's eyes with your own, and nothing intrigues the camera more than the eyes. (Even when your scene partner is off camera, they will be present to provide your "eye-line," and it will be possible for you to play to their eyes.)

Defining objectives will be easier after you have studied scene structure in the following chapter, but for now you can try to identify your character's objectives according to the principles we have discussed here.

Exercise 10.1: Productive Objectives

Examine your scene. Define your character's objectives as SIP. Try defining each as a change in your partner's eyes. Record and study the results.

Defining Playable Actions

In the Willy Loman scene, we described a productive objective: Willy enters and sees that the boss is busy; his single, immediate, and important objective is to get Howard's attention. Like any good writer, Miller has envisioned Willy's inner world and has provided an external action that springs naturally from this objective: Willy is going *to flatter* Howard. Although the action is provided by the writer, it is essential that you, the actor, "work backward" to discover it *for yourself*. You cannot simply accept the writer's result, you must recreate the whole process of thought and feeling which produces that result.

This is what Stanislavsky called *justifying* the external action by finding the inner need that drives it. Only in this way can you make the character's experience your own, and it is this experience that turns you into the character. When you find a way of understanding your character's action in a way that springs naturally from their objective, you have found what actor's call a *playable* action.

As you start out, it may help you to form a simple verbal description of each of your actions and objectives, step-by-step through a scene, in order to learn the best way of approaching the material. Eventually, this process will become largely intuitive, but for now, here are a few simple rules that will guide you in describing playable actions. First, use a *simple verb phrase* in a *transitive* form, that is, a verb that involves a *doing* directed toward someone else, such as "to flatter." Avoid forms of the verb "to be," since these are intransitive verbs; they have no external object and their energy turns back upon itself, certainly not a good condition for an actor whose energies must continually flow outward into the scene. You are never interested, for example, in "being angry" or "being a victim;" these are not playable actions.

Next, you select a verb that carries a sense of the *particular strategy* employed by the character to achieve the objective. When you choose a course of action in life, you naturally select the one that seems to offer the greatest chance for success in the given circumstances. You ask yourself, "Given what I want, what is the best way to get it in this situation, from this person? What might work?"

Here's how you might describe your action if you were playing Willy in the sample scene from *Death of a Salesman*. You have just entered; you desperately need to get a spot in town; you see Howard playing with the recorder. At this moment, you, as Willy, want to get Howard's attention (to get him to look at you), but you want to do it in a way that will make him feel positively towards you. As a salesman, you instinctively appeal to something the "client" is interested in, so you flatter him by praising the recorder and the stupid recording he has made of his family.

Obviously, you have a strong subtext here. You seem to be doing one thing, but you are actually trying to do something else, something that is, for the moment, hidden. You are also hiding your true feelings under a veneer of interest and cordiality. Though you are aware of this as an actor, as Willy you play the immediate objective (to get him to look at you) through the immediate action (flattery) while simply holding your true feelings in your hidden consciousness. As an actor, you avoid the temptation to "show" the audience what you are really feeling (which would be *indicating*) and simply trust your immediate action to carry all the hidden pain and impatience that lurks beneath it. (More about subtext in the following chapter.)

From these principles we see that the most complete description of what Willy is doing at this moment is *to flatter Howard by praising the recorder* (action) in order *to get him to look at me with interest* (objective). As useful as this verbal description may be at first, the ability to describe something (coming from the analytical left side of the brain) is no guarantee of the ability to play it (coming from the intuitive right side of the brain) and the two sometimes get in each other's way. You will soon discard such verbal descriptions in favor of an intuitive experience of the scene, moment by moment, having transferred your acting process completely into the creation of your character's consciousness.

Exercise 10.2: Playable Actions

Review your scene, and define each of your character's actions using a transitive verb phrase. Shoot the scene with this awareness, and study the results.

Spontaneity

What you do in front of the camera must be spontaneous, "for the first time," no matter how many times you have done it before. To achieve this spontaneity, you must keep your awareness on your objective rather than on the mechanics of your external action, just as the batter thinks only about the ball and not about his swing. Otherwise you will just be "going through the motions," repeating the external aspects of your performance without re-experiencing the internal needs that drive the externals.

Spontaneity does not mean that your performance is erratic or changeable: in order to maintain continuity between master and coverage, and from take to take, your action must have the same basic structure each time you perform it. During your preparation you have refined your understanding of the inner process of your character's thought until it becomes dependable and consistent; you live through that inner process in each take and allow yourself to "rediscover" the behavior which results. Just as the baseball batter has rehearsed his swing until he can do it without thinking, he then focuses all his attention on the particular ball coming at him. You will be free to pay full attention to the scene as it happens every time you do it. As Stanislavsky said,

> . . . a spontaneous action is one that, through frequent repetition in rehearsal and performance, has become automatic and therefore free."[1]

By re-experiencing the objective every time you perform the action, you will keep your performance spontaneous, even though it is also consistent and dependable. Review the tapes you have made of your scene so far; is your performance fresh and alive each time? You will have to repeat a scene many times when shooting a film.

---

[1]Stanislavsky, *An Actor's Handbook*, p. 138.

The Inner Monologue

We are now able to understand the entire flow of action from need to objective. In the opening of the scene from *Death of a Salesman,* Willy's inner thoughts might sound like this:

1. STIMULUS: What's that thing Howard's fooling with?
2. ATTITUDE: Why doesn't he stop that foolishness and listen to me?
3. ALTERNATIVES: I should demand the respect I'm entitled to.
4. CHOICE: But that might make him mad. I'd better get my foot in the door first, butter him up a bit.
5. ACTION: "What's that, Howard?"
6. OBJECTIVE: To get him to look at me with friendly eyes.

You can see that Willy's needs, values, way of thinking, way of relating to the world—in short, his entire psychology—is involved and expressed in each step of this mental process. Recreating your character's thought process in this way is the most important single step you can take toward transformation. One way to check the thoroughness and specificity of your psychological preparation is to verbalize your character's stream of consciousness as in the example above. This technique is called the *inner monologue.*

Exercise 10.3: The Inner Monologue

A. Work through your scene with your partner, speaking silently to yourself the inner stream of thought that connects the external things you do and say. Go slowly and allow yourself to experience each step in the flow from stimulus to choice to objective.

B. Select a portion of your scene in which your inner process of thought is especially rich. Shoot a close-up of yourself during this portion of the scene. See what the inner monologue has provided.

C. Finally, shoot a close master of your scene; don't try to keep the inner monologue going, just allow what you have learned from it to "be there." Study the result.

Summary

As you work on a scene, you discover your character's needs and the objectives he or she pursues to try to satisfy those needs. You define these objectives in a way that compels your attention and energizes you in a personal way, making them *productive objectives.* Remember the requirements of productive objectives as the acronym **SIP: Singular, Immediate,** and **Personal.** The best objective is *a change you want to bring about in the other character.*

These productive objectives lead to *playable actions.* To describe a playable action use a *simple verb phrase* in a *transitive form,* such as "to flatter." Avoid forms of the verb "to be," since these are intransitive verbs. As you start out, it may help to form such simple verbal descriptions of your actions and objectives, but eventually this process will become intuitive.

What you do in front of the camera must be spontaneous, "for the first time." You must keep your awareness on your objective rather than on the mechanics of your external action, just as the batter thinks only about the ball and not about his swing. By re-experiencing the objective every time you perform the action, you will keep your performance spontaneous, even though it is also consistent and dependable.

11 The Four Types of Outer Action

Once the choice to act has been made, your reaction turns into an outer, physical action—speech, movement, or both—directed toward an objective. As you can see in Figure 9.1, this outstroke can take four forms: it can be an *automatic action* that bypasses conscious choice; it can be a *direct action* that goes at the objective straightforwardly; it can be an *indirect action* that approaches the objective through some other activity; or it can be a *suppression,* a choice to do nothing. Let's examine each.

Automatic Actions

In an automatic action the stimulus results in an immediate physical response. For example, when you are riding in a car, your foot goes for the brake at the first sign of danger, even if you are not driving. Automatic actions include such "conditioned reflexes," as well as habits and impulses of many sorts. Much of a character's behavior is habitual: their speech, their walk, the way they wear their clothes, any special skills like handling a gun, running a computer, and so on. You should identify automatic aspects of the character's behavior as soon as possible, for they must become as natural and habitual to you as they are to your character.

The formation of new habits is accomplished best by regular, spaced repetition over a period of time, and this becomes homework to be done before coming to the set. Film actors, when they have sufficient advance notice, have sometimes gone to extraordinary lengths to learn special skills or develop certain qualities. Two famous examples are Robert De Niro's preparation for his role as a prize fighter in *Raging Bull* (for which he gained and lost sixty pounds) and the cast of *Apollo 13* undergoing astronaut training. It is neither necessary nor desirable for the habits of your character to invade your real life, but because the camera is so demanding, some film actors maintain certain habits—such as a dialect—throughout the shoot, even when they are off camera, for fear of being inconsistent when the camera is rolling.

Exercise 11.1: Automatic Actions

A. Review your scene; look for any habits, skills, or other automatic actions required of your character. Examine them to see what they tell you about your character. What program of homework can you establish to begin to develop these habits in yourself for this role? (If there are no automatic actions required in your scene, try creating some, such as performing it in a dialect.)

B. After a few days of preparation, shoot your scene. Study the tapes to see how well you have assimilated the automatic actions.

Automatic and non-automatic actions make different demands on you, and you must experience each in its own way. The general rule is: *Whatever your character doesn't need to think about, you shouldn't need to think about during shooting; and conversely, whatever your character does need to think about, you must think through each and every time you perform that action.*

Direct and Indirect Action: Subtext

Like people in real life, a character will usually choose an action that seems to have the best chance for success in the given circumstances, and when possible they will select a *direct* action such as persuading, demanding, cajoling, begging, and so on. However, when there is either an external or internal obstacle in the way of direct action, they will choose an *indirect* approach and hide their real objective beneath some other activity.

For example, if I want to tell you that I love you, but I am afraid that you will reject me (*internal obstacle*) I may choose instead to talk about how lonely I am, how dull the people I work with are, how you are the most interesting person I've met, the only one I feel comfortable with. All this is an indirect way of expressing my love "safely." (This is a scene from Chekhov's play, *The Three Sisters*. Chekhov explored indirect action more than any other writer, and his plays make excellent films.)

Or, if I want to tell you that I love you, but your husband is in the room with us (*external obstacle*), I may choose instead to talk about our pictures in the photo album, how wonderful you looked at the seashore last summer, what a wonderful time I had because you were there . . . whatever I think can be said without alerting your husband. (This is a scene from Ibsen's play, *Hedda Gabler*.) In both these examples the characters seem to be doing one thing (like looking at the photos) but are actually trying to do something else. The hidden action is called a *subtext* because it operates "underneath" the text.

In these examples, the characters were aware of their subtextual intentions. There may be situations, however, when a character is unconscious of their own subtext. For instance, in Tennessee Williams' play, *The Glass Menagerie*, a mother prepares her daughter for a "gentleman caller," but she also puts on her own party dress and hangs colored lights that will make her look younger. We realize that she unconsciously wants the gentleman caller for herself and is reliving her youth through her daughter.

When you recognize that your character has an unconscious subtext, there is a powerful temptation to bring it to the surface of the performance to make sure the audience doesn't miss it. This is a form of indicating and must be avoided at all cost. Whether conscious or unconscious, *subtext is always expressed through a surface activity*. Accept this surface activity as your immediate action and do *not* attempt to play the subtext. When actors make the mistake of bringing subtext to the surface, it destroys the reality of the scene. For one thing, if the audience can see the subtext, they may wonder why the other characters can't. In the case of unconscious subtext, in fact, it is best if you forget about it entirely (acting teacher Lee Strasberg once said that one of the hardest things about acting was "not knowing what you know.") Your simple awareness of the subtext is enough; trust that the camera will see it.

The subtle presence of subtext produces a richer performance; the camera sees that something is going on inside you, and this increases dramatic interest. Experience suggests that the actual content of the subtext may be irrelevant; *what* you are thinking is not as important as the fact that you *are* thinking. It may be a good idea, therefore, to invent a subtext even when there is no indirect action in the script. This needn't be a hidden objective; a hidden *attitude* toward the other character works just as well.

Exercise 11.2: Subtext

A. Examine your scene; look for any indirectly expressed or hidden objectives. Ask yourself:

1. Is the character conscious or unconscious of them?
2. Why can't they be expressed directly?
3. What surface activity has been provided through which they may be expressed?

B. If there is no indirect action in your scene, invent some hidden attitude or objective for yourself.

C. Shoot your scene with this awareness. Avoid playing the subtext. Study the tapes to see if the subtext has registered and if you have avoided bringing it to the surface.

Doing Nothing

As in life, a character may feel a need without immediately doing anything about it. The longer a need is delayed, the stronger it becomes. In Shakespeare's *Hamlet*, for example, the hero spends a great deal of time wondering whether or not to act upon his need to revenge his father's murder; his action explodes only in the last scene of the play.

Though we think of "doing nothing" as a passive act, it can actually be a strong form of action. This is because it takes more effort to hold an impulse in than it would to let it out. When this "holding in" is conscious, psychologists call it *suppression,* which literally means "pushing down." As you see in Figure 9.1, when a character chooses to suppress an impulse, that unresolved energy is reflected back into them and builds up to become a source of increasing dynamic tension. Suppression is common in drama because it heightens dramatic tension and suspense. Viewed in this way, there are no passive characters in drama, only characters who are aroused but then choose *not* to act. The ability to suppress an impulse is an important human capacity. One therapist says this about it:

> The delay between thought process and its translation into action is long enough to make it possible to inhibit it. The possibility of creating the image of an action and then delaying its execution is the basis for imagination and for intellectual judgement. . . . The possibility of delaying action, prolonging the period between the intention and its execution enables man to know himself.[1]

Suppression has many uses for the film actor. There is a short film showing the great film director Jean Renoir working with an actress in preparation for a highly emotional close-up. He sits her before the camera with the script and instructs her to read the words of her speech without emotion. She goes over the speech several times, and each time her natural response to the highly charged material starts to take over. At the slightest sign of emotion, however, Renoir sternly says, "No, no, just the words." You can literally see the emotional pressure rising in her as the suppressed responses struggle harder and harder to break free. Finally, when she is about to explode, Renoir calls "action" and the camera captures a splendid performance. Renoir's technique forced her to suppress her feelings until her inner dynamic had gotten so strong that they had to burst out. This can be an effective way of preparing that you can use for yourself.

In scenes in which the suppressed material is not released, your character is energized but doing nothing. A character in this state has a rich inner dynamic that is extremely interesting to the camera. Some film actors have this quality in their very presence, and it gives an edginess to their performance. They look as if they might do something drastic at any moment (James Woods and Jack Nicholson are examples).

If suppressed impulses are an important feature of a scene, one good way to prepare is to devote private rehearsal to letting the character do whatever it is they are suppressing. By giving yourself the experience of acting on

---

[1]Moshe Feldenkrais, *Awareness through Movement* (New York: Harper & Row, 1972), pp. 45–46.

the suppressed impulses, you force yourself to work harder to hold them in when you do the scene in its normal form. It is the effort to hold the impulse in that turns the "not doing" into a "doing" and makes it playable and dramatic.

So far we have been discussing conscious suppression. When the holding in of a response is *unconscious,* psychologists call it *repression* or *inhibition.* A repressed or inhibited character is not even aware that they are denying their impulses, but their behavior is affected anyway. Amanda in *The Glass Menagerie,* for example, is unconscious of the way she keeps her daughter dependent. If you recognize that your character is repressing something, you treat it in the same way you treat unconscious subtext; you "forget" about it and let your own unconscious processes do the rest. Remember this general rule: *strive to make your consciousness match that of your character, and "program" your unconscious through suggestion and rehearsal to match the character's unconscious as well.*

Exercise 11.3: Doings and Not Doings

If your scene contains some sort of outburst of feeling or action, use Renoir's technique of repeating that section of the scene over and over but suppressing the action until it forces itself out. On the other hand, if your scene contains consciously suppressed action, rehearse several times allowing the suppressed material to be released, then immediately repeat it for the camera and hold in the impulse. Or, if your character is unconsciously repressing something, identify it and then "forget" about it as you shoot the scene. Record these experiments and study the results.

Summary

Physical action can take four forms: *automatic action* that bypasses conscious choice; *direct action* that goes at the objective straightforwardly; *indirect action* that approaches the objective through some other activity; or the choice to *do nothing.*

Automatic actions are immediate physical responses, including habits and impulses of many sorts. Much of a character's behavior is automatic. Non-automatic actions may be either *direct,* or, when there is an external or internal obstacle, *indirect* in which the real objective is hidden beneath some other activity. The hidden action is called a *subtext.* Whether conscious or unconscious, *subtext is always expressed through a surface activity;* Do *not* attempt to play the subtext directly.

A character may also choose to do nothing. Though we think of "doing nothing" as a passive act, it can actually be a strong form of action. Viewed in this way, there are no passive characters in drama, only characters who are aroused but then choose *not* to act. When the holding in of a response is *unconscious,* psychologists call it *repression.* If you recognize that your character is repressing something, you treat it in the same way you treat unconscious subtext; you "forget" about it and let your own unconscious processes do the rest. Remember this general rule: *strive to make your consciousness match that of your character, and "program" your unconscious through suggestion and rehearsal to match the character's unconscious as well.*

CHAPTER

12 Dramatic Structure

As we do in life, characters will usually pursue an action until it either succeeds or fails. If it fails, they will shift to a different action, even though they may not change their objective; or they may abandon that objective and form a new one. On the other hand, if the action is successful and they achieve their objective, they move on to a new objective and form a new action.

Each change in action, whether there is a change of objective or not, can be felt as a change in the rhythm of the scene; each creates what Stanislavsky called a new "unit of action," regardless of which character has made the change. Actors usually call these units of action *beats,* and the moment in which the change of action occurs is called a *beat change.* (One theory about the origin of "beat" is the word "bit" said with a Russian accent, although a "beat," as in "downbeat," is a good description of the rhythmic quality of a well-shaped scene.)

In the scene from *Death of a Salesman,* for example, Willy tries several different ways to get a spot in town from Howard: by flattery, by appealing for sympathy, by appealing to loyalty, by appealing to honor, by generating guilt, and by demanding justice. Each of these actions is abandoned as it fails; each shift in action is a "beat change" and moves the scene in a new direction, even though Willy's overall objective changes only at the end, when he tries to save his job by begging.

Most important, notice that *within each beat, your character has a single action and objective.* It is this fact that permits you to translate the architecture of the scene into the thoughts and actions of your character. You, as the actor, understand this structure and design the consciousness of the character so as to reflect it. Then, as you play the scene, you can surrender your complete awareness to the character's consciousness, secure in the knowledge that what your character thinks, says, and does will serve the scene.

If all the actors have worked together to develop a shared understanding of the architecture of the scene, the rhythm of the scene will be strong and clear. It is as important for actors to agree on the phraseology of their shared action as it is for members of an orchestra to work together to fulfill the phraseology of a piece of music. In practice, this is done quickly and most often intuitively in the initial read-throughs, without overt discussion. All the actors are looking for the rhythm of the scene, feeling where the beats change, as if they were dancing with one another.

It makes it easier to define beats if you remember that a *beat always changes at the moment one of the characters chooses to pursue a new action.* Some of these choices may be significant enough to affect the plot of the story as a whole, and these demand special attention; there will usually be only one such special choice in each scene. In the sample scene from *Cheers*, for example, Carla's main choice is to not marry Ben, and Ben's main choice is to accept Carla's rejection with grace. Everything that is said and done in the scene either leads to or flows from these two crucial choices, and they are the heart of the entire show.

The Shape of Drama

All dramatic events have a similar shape, and this shape is basically the same in beats, scenes, and entire stories. It is critically important that you understand this shape because as a film actor you will work piece by piece and must ensure that each piece will fit into the whole.

In a dramatic story, the sequence of events (the plot) moves forward as suspense builds; we begin to wonder, "How will this come out?" When the question is just on the verge of being answered, suspense is at its peak. This moment of greatest suspense is called the *crisis* ("turning point"). Everything that happens before the crisis leads toward it with rising tension, while everything after the crisis flows naturally from it with a falling sense of resolution (or *denouement,* which is the French word for "unraveling").

This, then, is the fundamental shape of all dramatic events: rising tension leading to a crisis, followed by a resolution (see Figure 12.1). It is a shape common to all of the performing arts; along with plays and films, symphonies and ballets also have it. It is the fundamental unit of rhythm because it is the shape of a muscular contraction and relaxation. It is the fundamental shape of life itself from birth to death. You can even experience it within a single breath.

Exercise 12.1: A Dramatic Breath

You can experience the shape of drama in a single breath. Start as "empty" as you can: feel the rising energy (inhaling); prolong the crisis (holding the breath) and feel the holding of the breath as a moment of suspense; then enjoy a full resolution (exhaling). A single breath can be an exciting event.

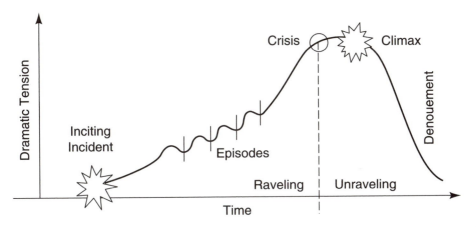

FIGURE 12.1   The Shape of Drama.

In this exercise you heightened the "drama" of the breath in two ways: you extended its dynamic range (what we call its *arc*) by stretching the low and high points of the action farther apart; you also *prolonged the crisis* so as to savor the period of maximum suspense. These same principles will apply to the shaping of an entire story, a scene, and the beats within a scene.

Story Architecture

The various pieces of your performance must work together to create a unified whole even though they are shot in small pieces and usually out of sequence. Your sense of the overall "architecture" of the performance must be rock solid to guide you in approaching each of the small pieces as you shoot. We can best illustrate this sense of architecture with a physical exercise.

Exercise 12.2: Story Architecture

Perform the following sequence of simple actions, attempting to fully experience the dramatic potential of each. Remember to focus on the crisis in each pattern: treat all that goes before as leading up to the crisis and all that follows as flowing from it.

A. A single footstep. Where is the crisis of a footstep? To intensify the experience, involve your breath by inhaling during the rising action, holding the breath during the crisis, and exhaling during the release.

B. Three footsteps experienced as one phrase, with the crisis in the third step. The first two steps still have mini-crises of their own, but now they lead up to the main crisis in the third step. Let your breath parallel the larger pattern.

C. Three footsteps with the crisis in the first step, so that the mini-crises of the second and third steps will flow as a resolution from the first.

D. Now try a pattern composed of three units of three footsteps each, with the crisis of the whole pattern in the last unit of three (see Figure 6.2).

In this exercise you experienced how a number of small units of action (like breaths or steps) can be connected into a larger phrase having a shape of its own. Likewise, these larger phrases can be connected into still larger patterns that again have shapes of their own. On all these levels, the fundamental shape of rise, crisis, and release is the same, even though the proportion or relationship between the parts may be different on each level (see Figure 12.2).

This is how the parts of a film go together to comprise the whole. The beats work together to form scenes, and the scenes flow toward the main event of the story as a whole. This architecture is not an arbitrary choice made by the actors: it is built into the script by the writer. Each actor works to recognize the structure provided in the whole, in each scene, and in each beat.

Most stories are driven by some *main conflict*; the simplest kind of conflict is between the main characters, the protagonist (hero) and the antagonist (villain), though sometimes the main conflict can live within the central character. Each scene also has a *scene conflict* that is an aspect of the main conflict, and each beat contains an *immediate conflict* which is a step in the working out of the scene conflict.

In *Miss Evers' Boys*, for example, the *main conflict* is within Miss Evers, between her love for her patients and her sense of duty to the doctors as a nurse. In our sample scene, the *scene conflict* is over the fate of the men whom the doctors intend to allow to die. The *immediate conflict* at the opening of the

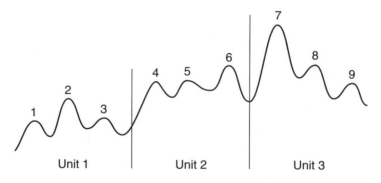

FIGURE 12.2 Compound Rhythms. Here, nine steps shaped as three units combine to produce one large pattern.

scene is between Evers and Douglas as she demands penicillin, and he counters with, "It cannot cure and it may kill." Identifying the relationship between the main, scene, and immediate conflicts in this way can help you to see how each part of the story fits into the whole.

Scene Structure

Scenes are structured like miniature plays: each has its own scene conflict and its own crisis. A scene will not usually have much resolution, however, because it must propel us into the next scene; if it does not, the story will seem too "episodic." In the scene from *Miss Evers' Boys*, for example, nothing is resolved after Nurse Evers makes her emotional exit, and Brodus' last line, "Let me talk to her," leads us directly into the next scene.

Each scene contains one major development in the movement of the whole story. This development may be an event which is one link in the chain of the plot; it may be a major change in relationship, or it may be a major thematic development. In any case, every scene contains a "milestone" in the progress of the entire story, and identifying it will give your work a sense of priority and purpose.

You can identify a scene's function by asking yourself, "If this scene were cut, what would be lost that would damage the plot? What would be lost from the meaning of the story?" In the scene from *Miss Evers' Boys*, the milestone is the word "autopsy," the revelation that the doctors intend to let the men die without treatment.

Each beat within the scene has an *immediate* conflict that is a step in the working out of the scene conflict. Like a scene, a beat will not have a strong resolution since that would interrupt the momentum of the scene; rather, *the resolution of one beat begins the rising action of the next*. For this reason, it is difficult to say where one beat ends and another begins since the end of one *is* the beginning of the next. It is easier and more specific to say where the moment of crisis is in each beat; this is the *beat change*. Beats change when one of the characters forms a new action, causing a counteraction in the other character, thus the structure of the scene is inextricably tied to the thoughts and feelings of the characters.

Having come to understand the structure of the scene in this way, you are free during performance to keep your focus on the immediate objective, playing moment by moment, knowing that each moment will serve its beat, the beat will serve the scene, and the scene will serve the film as a whole. This is especially important when you are shooting out of chronological sequence.

It may be useful for you to prepare an outline of the beats of the scene; this is called a *scene breakdown*. One easy way to do this is by marking the beat changes in your script. Though you may analyze the scene's structure intellectually in this way at first, experienced actors eventually approach structure intuitively, developing a shared rhythmic experience of the rise and fall of the scene's energy. Your sense of scene structure must finally live as an underlying "dance" in the flow of the scene.

Most important, your understanding of the beat structure of the scene will reveal that the sequence of your character's objectives has a logic of its own that can carry you through the scene with a sense of continuity and momentum. Stanislavsky called this flow from objective to objective the *score* of the role. He described it like this:

> An actor becomes so accustomed to all his objectives and their sequence that he cannot conceive of approaching his role otherwise than along the line of the steps fixed in the score. . . . The score automatically stirs the actor to physical action.[1]

You are developing this score from your very first reading of the scene, and you strive to assimilate it until it becomes part of you, an "inner model" that becomes the "map" for your journey through the scene.

Exercise 12.3: Scene Structure

A. Working with your partner, answer these questions about your scene:

1. How does this scene cause the plot to progress? How does it enhance the meaning of the story?
2. What is the central conflict of the scene?

B. Do a breakdown of the beats of the scene.

C. Decide which beat contains the crisis of the scene. How do all the previous beats flow toward it, and how do subsequent beats flow from it?

D. Translate the structure of the scene into the inner thought process of your character, thereby developing the score of the scene.

E. Shoot the scene and study the result. Can you feel the shape of the scene as it flows from beat to beat?

The Superobjective

In the first beat of the scene from *Death of a Salesman*, Willy's *immediate objective* is to get Howard's attention. He would then hope to move toward his *scene objective* which is to persuade Howard to give him a spot in town. This scene objective is connected directly to his life goal, which we call his *superobjective: to prove himself a worthy human being by earning money and respect.*

---

[1]Stanislavsky, *Creating a Role*, p. 62. Used with the permission of the publisher, Theatre Arts Books, 153 Waverly Place, New York, NY 10014.

(Notice that the superobjective is described in the same way as all other objectives, by a transitive verb phrase.)

If we were to follow each of Willy's immediate objectives throughout the story, we could see how he is led from objective to objective in pursuit of his superobjective. Stanislavsky put it this way:

> The whole stream of individual minor objectives, all the imaginative thoughts, feelings and actions of [the character] should converge to carry out this super-objective.[2]

Your character's superobjective may be conscious or (more commonly) unconscious. If the character is unconscious of his or her superobjective, you will treat it as you treat everything you know that the character doesn't— you will take it into account as you shape the inner life of the character, but in performance you will "forget it" and simply allow it to operate, not letting your actor awareness contaminate your character reality.

Conscious or unconscious, the superobjective functions as an underlying principle that affects all your character's actions and establishes his or her attitude toward life. Each scene, each beat, each moment of the role, and every aspect of your character's psychology can be understood as reflecting this superobjective.

When playing a minor character, it may be difficult and perhaps unnecessary to find the superobjective because the writer probably has not provided much information about the character. Here you can be inventive as long as what you develop enables you to accurately serve your dramatic function within the story as a whole.

Once you have identified the superobjective, you must personalize it and feel it as deeply as does your character. Since the superobjective of most characters is fairly "universal," this is usually not difficult. For example, like Willy Loman, we all want to be thought of as valuable, and we can all identify with Willy on this basis, even though we can see that Willy's way of pursuing self-esteem is mistaken. Identifying how your character's immediate objectives arise from their superobjective can help you to better shape each beat as you shoot it so that it will fit into the arc and flow of the whole performance.

Exercise 12.4: The Superobjective

Considering the whole script from which your scene comes, answer these questions:

A. Can you see a superobjective toward which all your character's actions tend, whether they are conscious of it or not? Define the superobjective using a transitive verb phrase.

[2]Stanislavsky, *An Actor's Handbook*, p. 56.

B. Find something in your own life which allows you to personalize this superobjective, so that you feel it with the same intensity as does your character.

C. Shoot your scene again and watch to see how the superobjective is expressed in it.

Summary

A story is structured on several levels: beats make up scenes, and the scenes form the overall shape of rising and falling action that give unity to the whole story. These levels of action relate directly to the inner life of your character because you will have an action directed toward an objective on each level. In each beat you have an *immediate* objective, and the sequence of immediate objectives (the score) leads toward your *scene* objective. In turn, your scene objectives can be seen as springing from a deeper, overall objective that is your character's "life goal" or, as it is usually called, their *superobjective*.

CHAPTER

13 Emotion

Stanislavsky understood that actors often need to produce emotion on demand. In fact, he modeled his system of acting after a great opera singer who was able to deliver the emotional fullness of a moment at the precise time required by the music. There is even a story that he once brought a trapeze artist into his school to teach the actors that when it was time to jump, they had to jump. For the film actor, the moment to jump is when the director calls, "Action!" Your emotional technique has to support you as you take that leap. You can begin to build this technique by understanding the various ways emotion functions in real life and by heightening your sensitivity to each of these natural emotional processes.

There are three schools of thought in psychology about the way emotion functions: one is that our emotions are judgements that we pass on our actions; another is that they are part and parcel of our physical state; yet a the third is that they arise from our thoughts and attitudes. All three are true at various times, and all three can be useful to the film actor.

Working from the Outside In

Two of the theories of emotion focus on the way you respond to the external world and your relationship to it. The first is that your emotions spring from your judgement of your efforts to get something you want: if you get it, you're *happy*, if you don't, you're *sad*. If you don't get what you want and it's not your fault, you feel *angry*. When you don't get what you want and you don't know why, you feel *afraid*. When you don't know what you want, you feel *helpless*. If you can experience your character's needs as if they were your own, this process will work for you automatically.

A second view of emotion was developed by two early psychologists, Fritz Lange and William James; we know that Stanislavsky was familiar with it. This theory holds that emotion is an integral part of your bodily condition when you respond to some external stimulus. Imagine, for example, that you are stepping off a curb when, out of the corner of your eye, you see a car rush-ing toward you. Immediately you leap back out of danger. You did not jump because you were afraid—there wasn't time for that. Your body responded automatically, and only after you had jumped clear, with your heart pound-ing, adrenaline flowing, and your breath short, did you recognize your own condition and call it "fear." Your emotion did not cause your action, your action caused your emotion.

Exercise 13.1: Emotion through Physical Action

In *Death of a Salesman*, Arthur Miller vividly describes Willy's physical condition in his first entrance:

> From the right, Willy Loman, the Salesman, enters, carrying two large sample cases. . . . He is past sixty years of age, dressed quietly. Even as he crosses the stage to the doorway of the house, his exhaustion is apparent. He unlocks the door, comes into the kitchen, and thankfully lets his burden down, feeling the sore-ness of his palms. A word-sigh escapes his lips—it might be "Oh, boy, oh, boy."

Perform this physical action, just as Miller describes it. Surrender yourself to the experience. How did it make you feel?

This physical pattern by itself is powerful enough to generate an emo-tional state in you if you perform it with full participation of body and mind. As Plato noted two thousand years ago, the actor mimicking the gestures of an angry person tends to become angry. This idea encouraged the American director William Ball to tell his actors to "do the act and the feeling will fol-low." Even Stanislavsky, later in life, began to work from the outside in through what he called the "Method of Physical Actions."

Because feeling will follow from a fully felt physical action, your own emotional response to what you are doing in a scene can guide you in check-ing the correctness of your action. This is what the experienced actor means when they try something and then say, "It didn't feel right." When you find the correct action, the correct feeling will follow. Again, this process is auto-matic and requires only that you be fully engaged and committed to your action.

Working from the Inside Out

The third idea of emotion is that it is generated by your thoughts, expecta-tions and attitudes. The school of psychotherapy called "cognitive therapy" is based on this idea:

> The first principle of cognitive therapy is that all your moods are created by your "cognitions," or thoughts. A cognition refers to the way you look at things—

your perceptions, mental attitudes, and beliefs. It includes the way you inter-pret things—what you say about something or someone to yourself. You feel the way you do right now because of the thoughts you are thinking at this moment. . . . The moment you have a certain thought and believe it, you will experience an immediate emotional response. Your thought actually creates the emotion.[1]

For example, suppose you are reading this thinking, "Hey, that sounds good; Benedetti's approach could really help me." This positive thought will make you feel good. If, on the other hand, you are thinking, "This is too hard, I could never do it," then your feeling will be negative and sad.

Psychologists who treat depression have noticed that depressed peo-ple are seldom less successful in objective terms than many who are not depressed; the difference lies more in the way they subjectively view them-selves and their lives. They "send themselves messages" that are negative, and every hint of failure confirms this negative self-attitude. Willy Loman, for example, is constantly sending himself the message that he is unworthy and has to earn the respect of others. Willy has accepted the materialistic atti-tude of his society and measures his personal worth in external terms: when the size of his paycheck and the smiles of his clients diminish, he feels dimin-ished as a person.

Psychotherapists have found that if depressed people can identify their negative self-messages and replace them with realistically positive ones, they can change the way they feel. This proves that emotion can indeed arise from patterns of thought. The actor can use this same process to develop the emo-tional life of the character by examining the character's patterns of thought and especially their attitude toward themselves. Ask yourself: What is my character's dominant self-image? What messages does my character send to himself or herself?

Exercise 13.2: Emotion from the Inside Out: Self-Image

A. Enter into your character's frame of mind just as your scene begins, and complete these phrases:

1. The most beautiful part of my body is . . .
2. Happiness to me is . . .
3. The thing I most want to do before I die is . . .
4. The ugliest part of my body is . . .
5. Pain to me is . . .
6. The most secret thing about me is . . .
7. I can hear my father's voice speaking through my own when I tell myself . . .

[1]David D. Burns, *Feeling Good* (New York: Signet, 1980), pp. 11–12.

8. Love to me is . . .
9. If you could hear the music in me . . .
10. I want my epitaph to be . . .

B. Immediately shoot the scene and allow these feelings to affect what you do. Study the results.

As you see, emotion arises *automatically* out of your involvement in both the actions *and* thoughts of your character. Hopefully this will persuade you that you needn't be concerned with emotional behavior as such. If you enter fully into the character's inner life and external actions, emotion will arise automatically. *You should never be concerned with playing emotion.*

Emotion Memory and Substitution

As you begin to participate fully in the actions and thoughts of your character, you will begin to have associations and memories of similar situations from your own past life. Connecting this personal material with the character's situation can enrich the performance tremendously. Stanislavsky experimented with the idea that the actor could develop a wealth of emotion memories as a resource for the acting process, much as a painter learns to mix colors:

> The broader your emotion memory, the richer your material for inner creativeness. . . . Our creative experiences are vivid and full in direct proportion to the power, keenness and exactness of our memory. . . . Sometimes memories continue to live in us, grow and become deeper. They even stimulate new processes and either fill out unfinished details or suggest altogether new ones.[2]

One idea from early Russian psychology that appealed to Stanislavsky was that every cell in the body has a capacity for memory, so that memories of emotional states live in the body as well as in the mind. Several contemporary schools of psychology would agree; people undergoing deep massage often discover vivid emotional experiences stored in specific areas of the body. The school of therapy called Bioenergetics explains this by pointing out that repeated patterns of behavior alter the very structure of the body. Eventually, the altered body structure becomes a permanent "character armor," a physical manifestation of personality and emotion.

There may be times when you will want to evoke a stored memory as a way of personalizing and enriching your connection with your character. One technique is called *Visuo-Motor Behavior Rehearsal:* By relaxing deeply and entering into a visualization of your character's situation, allowing your deep

[2]Stanislavsky, *An Actor's Handbook,* p. 56.

muscles to respond freely to the visualization, you can invite associations from your store of memories. These associations, or *recalls,* will then automatically become attached to the character's actions and situation. It is neither necessary nor desirable to "play" them; they are simply allowed to "be there."

Another memory technique that may be useful in certain situations involves making a mental *substitution* of a person, place, or situation from your own life for one in the scene. Such a substitution is a special kind of emotion memory and will often arise naturally as you work. If, for instance, you are supposed to be terribly afraid of another character, you might be reminded of someone frightening from your own life and substitute him or her in your own mind for that character. In an example from the ancient theater, a famous Greek actor, in a scene about a father learning of the death of his son, had the ashes of his real son (who had died recently) brought to him on stage. Recalls and substitutions needn't be rooted in real events; your fantasies can often supply more powerful material than real events. In either case, the personal involvement provided by these techniques can sometimes be invaluable for the film actor.

As useful as emotion memory and substitution may sometimes be, however, they must be used with caution. First, while recalls may be useful for opening an initial connection into the character's experience, you must go beyond this initial connection into the *specific* experience of your character within his or her given circumstances. If you do not, your response may be merely personal without being appropriate to the demands of the scene. Second, memories can carry very powerful emotions, and those that have not yet been fully integrated can easily overwhelm you and draw you out of the scene. There is also a danger that the emotional power of memory may distract you from your focus on your objective and action and lure you into playing an emotional state. Because of these inherent dangers, Stanislavsky himself eventually abandoned these techniques.

Since memories and associations arise naturally in the course of preparing a role, not much is gained by using them in a premeditated way. Perhaps the best strategy is to remain open to recalls and substitutions that arise naturally in the course of your work, but avoid holding them in your awareness as you perform; simply allow them to "be there." Though recalls may be used as a last resort when all other efforts to meet the demands of a scene have failed, some film actors find more direct and immediate techniques sometimes produce better results. It is said that Robert De Niro, when once preparing for a scene in which he was to experience great pain, simply ran around with a rock in his shoe just before the take.

Exercise 13.3: Emotion Recalls and Substitutions

A. In some private place, relax and go through your scene mentally: put yourself in your character's situation and live through their actions as if you were actually doing them in those circumstances. Let your body respond freely. As you live through the scene, notice the emotional associations that arise. Do you remember events from your past? Do the other characters remind you of people you have known?

B. Now examine the most significant of these memories. Ask yourself the following questions:

1. How does it make me feel about myself? About the other people in this memory?
2. Are there ideas, attitudes, or beliefs connected with this memory?
3. Do I recall making any choices at this time, even unconsciously, that have affected me since?
4. Are there images from even earlier times contained in this memory? If so, experience these: continue to allow such images to flood up and take you back further and further in time.

C. Review this experience and evaluate any connections that were made. Are they useful to the scene? Do they need to be specified or altered to meet the exact demands of the character or scene?

D. Shoot your scene and simply allow these associations to "be there." Study the result. Did your emotional recalls enrich your performance? Did they draw you away from your action by encouraging you to play an emotional state? Are there any more direct and immediate techniques which could help you to prepare more effectively?

Summary

Emotion can result from our actions depending on whether we feel we have been successful or unsuccessful; they can result from physical changes in our body caused by our actions; and they can be triggered by our thoughts and the messages we send ourselves. All these approaches function automatically and can be useful to the film actor, as can the techniques of emotional recall and substitution. However, whether you work from the outside in, from the inside out, or simultaneously both ways you need never play emotion for its own sake.

CHAPTER

14 Starting a Career in Film and Television

Before you decide to commit to a career in film and television, there are some facts you should consider. According to statistics from the Screen Actors Guild, in 1996 more than 85 percent of SAG's ninety thousand members earned less than $5,000 a year under a SAG contract, and more than 25 percent earned nothing. As you start out, then, it would be wise to have enough savings to live for two years with no income. Even once you start to get work, you will probably need a "day job" that has a schedule flexible enough to allow you to go to auditions, often with very little advance warning. Jobs like telemarketing, waiting tables, and part-time teaching are popular with beginning actors.

Assuming that the financial risk doesn't stop you and you determine to pursue a professional career as a film and television actor, your next question may well be, "Where should I live?" The conventional answer used to be, "For theater go to New York, but for film and television you must go to Los Angeles." This, however, is not entirely true nowadays. First of all, the competition in Los Angeles is fierce. Of the ninety-six thousand members of SAG in 1999, about forty-six thousand live in Southern California. Of these, probably 95 percent are unemployed on any given day. Second, because of lower labor costs, favorable rates of exchange, and special tax incentives, there are now more shows of all types being done outside of Los Angeles than in it (except for sitcoms).

The most active cities for "runaway production" are Toronto, Vancouver, New York, Atlanta, Charlotte, Wilmington, Orlando, and Chicago. A good actor living in one of these cities can do very well with a minimum of competition. Of course, these "local hires" don't get the biggest roles because they lack name recognition; so while you can make a decent part-time living and do good work outside of Los Angeles, you can't be a full-time actor, much less a star. Nevertheless, it may be better to develop experience and credits while living somewhere else *before* you make an assault on Los Angeles.

Getting Started

In whatever city you begin your career, your first step should be to start *networking*. Get in touch with other actors, old friends, whoever's around, join a membership theatre that does good work (avoid amateurish groups), take reputable professional classes, hang out where you can meet people in the business. Call the alumni association at your college, find out who from your school is in the business, and don't be shy about asking for help. Subscribe to the local "trade papers." If you have to take a job to support yourself, try to get a job, any job, in the industry, including working as a production assistant, an extra, an intern, whatever. It is important to be "around" as much as you can and to get current information about the business. Being in the right place at the right time can be the key to a career break.

At the same time, start trying to get yourself seen: most cities have non-union theater groups, like the Actors waiver theaters (seating 99 or less) permitted by the Actors Equity Association in Los Angeles. Audition for as many shows as you can; the auditioning itself is good experience and helps to build your network. Act in non-union and student films, and be sure to have all the work you do compiled on your "reel"; having a reel is a tremendous advantage in getting an agent. If there is a reputable showcase operation in your city, give it a try. For a modest cost, these operations develop programs of auditions by a group of actors and invite agents and casting directors. In the case of both classes and showcases, however, beware: there are some very disreputable people in this business. Be especially wary of so-called "talent placement services," and anyone who guarantees you work.

Early on, you will want to prepare your *photo and resume*. Look at the "head shots" of other actors until you see one you really like; find out who took it, what the photo session was like, and how much it cost. Though this is a job that can be done by a talented friend, a professional will usually produce better results. You will want your photo to give an appealing and honest sense of your real appearance: avoid overly glamorous or sexy shots, and avoid also shots that convey a strong mood or emotion—these are limited in their usefulness. Your headshots can be duplicated at low cost in batches of one hundred or more at various photo labs, with your name in the margin if you wish. See your Yellow Pages or ads in the trade papers.

Your resume may be pretty short at this point. Don't be ashamed of listing college or little theater credits. Specify your training experience, listing names of teachers if they might be known in the business.

Getting an Agent

Eventually, you will need to get an **agent.** You can't usually audition for a union job unless you are submitted by a franchised agent, so be sure any agent you consider is franchised; you can get a list of franchised agents from the SAG office in your area or from the SAG web site. Remember that no reputable agent will ever charge you in advance: they make their money *only* from the 10 percent commission they receive *when they find you work*, and not before. (About managers: only big stars need personal managers. If someone offers to be your manager, decline.)

Getting an agent is very difficult in Los Angeles, a little easier in other cities. There are reputable agents in most of the cities I listed previously, some of whom may be directly or indirectly affiliated with agencies in Los Angeles. An agent may agree to represent you "informally" at first, without first asking you to sign an agency agreement and before you are a member of a union (you will be able to join a union if you get an offer of union work). The agent may send you out on a few auditions to see if you make a good impression; this is a reasonable strategy for a newcomer. Be thankful if you find an agent willing to take you on in this way.

One common way of getting an agent is by *being seen* on stage or in a showcase. Whenever you are going to appear somewhere, be sure to send out cards with a photograph to agents and casting directors, and get on the phone to everyone you know. **Casting directors** can be very important to you, and they have an organization of their own called the Casting Society of America (CSA). Many casting directors were once actors themselves, and most of them are wonderful people who are often more diligent about going to see new talent in the showcases and little theatres than are agents.

Even if you aren't performing somewhere, you might *mail out a photo and resume* to that list of franchised agents you got from SAG. In some cities, you may find a service that sells mailing lists of agents and casting directors on gummed labels, or you may find such lists for sale at big photocopying shops or at bookstores specializing in film and theater books. Follow up your mailing with phone calls, and try to set up personal meetings. Don't pin too much hope on your mailings, however; they have very limited effectiveness and work best as back-up to a personal recommendation, a role in a play, a personal meeting, or some other strategy.

Joining a Union

You should not join a union until you are confident that your career has indeed gotten underway. First, being in the union in no way guarantees that you will get work. Second, every union has what SAG calls "Rule One:" no union member may accept ANY non-union acting work. This means that once you join, you are cutting yourself off from amateur, community, or school work that might give you needed experience (though you may be able to get permission to act in certain student films). Nor is it necessary to join a union as soon as you get union work. The federal Taft-Hartley law requires that a non-union actor may be hired under a union contract for thirty days before he or she must join the union. So make this choice with care, and don't necessarily jump at union membership as soon as it is available.

Perhaps the easiest unions to join are the theater union, Actor's Equity Association **(AEA),** and the Screen Extras Guild (SEG). For dancers and singers, there is both the American Guild of Musical Artists (AGMA) and the American Guild of Variety Artists (AGVA). These unions are all affiliated with AFTRA and SAG. The advantage of first joining one of these affiliated unions is that it may make it easier to join AFTRA or SAG later, and your initiation fee and dues will be less. Professional work in the live theater is an especially good precursor to a film or television career, both for the experience and the contacts it will give you.

You can join **AFTRA,** which has jurisdiction over taped television shows and radio, by simply paying the initiation fee (around $800) and first year's dues (around $45). This is not really necessary, however, because you can get an AFTRA job without being a member and will then have thirty days during which you can work without joining. If you want to go on working after that, you will have to join.

Most film actors want eventually to join the Screen Actors Guild **(SAG).** Joining SAG can be something of a "Catch 22": You can't join unless you have an offer of employment from a company that has signed the SAG business agreement, and you can't usually audition for such companies unless you are a member of SAG. There are two exceptions: if you have been a member of one of the affiliated guilds listed earlier for at least one year and have worked as a "principal" at least once, or if you work as an extra in a SAG project at full SAG rates for three days, you may then join SAG without an offer of employment, and your initiation fee may be reduced from the usual rate of about $1,200 plus the annual minimum dues of about $100. As difficult as all this may sound, thousands of people find some way to join SAG every year. For more information and many valuable tips, as well as a list of franchised agents, visit the excellent SAG web site at http://www.sag.org.

Above all, remember this sage advice from Kirk Douglas:

> The important thing I've learned is not that you want your kids to be successful, but that you want them to be happy. Happiness doesn't always equate with success. That's why I've always discouraged my kids from ever going into my profession."[1]

The Casting Process

There are actually three different processes for casting a show: one for the stars, one for principal supporting roles, and one for the "day players" who

---

[1]Quoted in the SAG web site.

play the smaller roles. The casting of stars is as much an economic as a creative decision. The financing of feature films, or the final approval of television movies or sitcoms by a network or cable company, is always contingent on casting. The producers must provide "name" players for the principal roles who, in the opinion of the financing entity, will attract a sufficient audience to justify the cost of production and distribution. The banks which specialize in financing feature films have ideas about the value of various actors (one actor may be more "bankable" than another), and networks and cable companies have ideas about which actors are best for their particular audience.

The casting of stars begins only when the script has been approved for production. The casting director makes lists of the available possibilities to be considered by the financing entity, the producers, and the director. Eventually all of these people agree on a choice, and an offer is made to the actor's agent. Auditions for the major roles are rarely held, since a well-established actor is not usually expected to audition. Instead, the script is sent to the actor to be read. Not all offers are accepted, and often several actors have to be approached before a deal is closed. (I once produced a television movie in which offers were made to seventeen actors before the starring role was finally cast.)

Only when the stars have been set does the show get the **green light.** Now the principal supporting roles, usually three to six in number, are cast to round out the "marquee" of the show. Again, the casting director makes lists and the whole process repeats itself. These are also name actors, or "hot" young actors, and auditions are held only if there is some question about the choice and the actor is willing.

A few weeks before shooting is to start, the casting of the **day players** begins. Some of these roles can be quite good, can work many days if not weeks, but don't require a name actor. *These are the roles you will be trying to win as you begin your career.* The casting director sends a **breakdown,** a brief description of each available part, to the agents in the area. Your agent looks at the breakdown as soon as it arrives and submits the photo and resume of his or her clients who seem most appropriate for each role. The casting director reviews these and decides which actors should be called in for a preliminary audition.

If the show is shooting outside Los Angeles, a **local casting director** is hired to cast the day players in that area. This person does the initial screening, sometimes calling in specific actors they know who might be right for various parts. Three to six finalists are selected for each role, and their auditions are put on videotape. The videotapes are sent for review by the director and the producers. Sometimes casting may be done directly from these tapes; other times, **callbacks** will be held for the most promising candidates after the director arrives on location. If you are living outside Los Angeles, the local casting directors are tremendously important to you.

Commercials, Industrials, and Looping

Besides movies, sitcoms, and soap operas, there are two other venues in which an actor can find gainful employment: *commercials* and *industrial shows.* Industrials are shows created for specific companies or events such as annual meetings, conventions, product launches, and so on. These shows often involve special skills like singing and dancing. They are produced by companies which specialize in this kind of work, and forming a relationship with such a company can be a valuable source of ongoing employment.

Commercials use a tremendous number of actors, and fresh faces are always welcome. Appearing in a national commercial that runs for some period of time can be very lucrative, though recent changes in the commercial pay structure have made them less so than at one time. Commercial auditions are usually arranged by agents who specialize in this, and some actors have both a theatrical and a commercial agent. If you decide to go into commercials, you should get a special composite photo prepared by a photographer with experience in the commercial field. These composites usually have an attractive general 8″ x 10″ photo on one side, and a number of smaller photos showing you in various situations and "looks" on the other.

Pursuing a commercial career can be very time-consuming, as you must expect to make a great many auditions in order land a job. The waiting time at commercial auditions is often longer than for theatrical auditions, even though the audition itself is likely to be very brief, sometimes frustrating, or even silly. Most commercial auditions are videotaped; if a script is involved it will be displayed on a large cue card. Your skill in reading from cue cards without appearing to do so can be important, but since the text is usually brief you may choose to memorize instead. If you do, however, be aware that the words of a commercial are treated as if they were holy writ, and word-perfect delivery is required.

Becoming a member of a *looping group*—one of the groups which supplies crowd noise and other vocal embellishments (**"walla"**) for films—can be a good source of regular employment. Since the composition of these groups is determined by the needs of each project, they have some flexibility that can permit their members to take other acting jobs as they arise. Some vocal flexibility is useful, but not essential. This specialty is available only in those cities where a significant amount of post-production is done, namely Los Angeles, New York, and Toronto.

Likewise, voice work for cartoons and radio commercials in the same cities provides good employment for a small number of actors. Seek out an agent who specializes in this area, and get help in creating a voice reel that entertainingly presents a range of vocal characters.

Auditions

Auditions are a nerve-wracking but necessary part of the actor's life. When you are called to audition, your agent will notify you, often only one day— sometimes a few hours—in advance. This is one of the reasons why you must be reachable by telephone at all times: don't depend on answering machines, friends, relatives, or co-workers to pass on messages, but consider a cell phone or less expensive beeper.

Casting directors will often put the scenes to be read for each role in envelopes on their office doors the day before the audition, and you can stop by and pick them up. Otherwise, arrive early enough to look over the material and prepare. In addition to the scenes provided by the casting director, the union requires that the entire script must be available to you on request, but it is rarely worth the time to read it; the description in the breakdown should give you as much information as you need to prepare. If you have important questions about motivation or the character's function in the show, you can ask at the audition. There are special classes on auditioning available, and if you can find a reputable one, it may well be worth your while; the cost may be tax-deductible.

At the audition, dress neatly and appropriately to the material you will perform, but not in a "costume." Your agent will probably have already sent your photo and resume, but bring them with you just in case. When you arrive at the audition, you will first sign in and get the material if you haven't already. Since you are early, you can go off to prepare. Your immediate job is to find a productive objective and playable action in the material and to make that objective important to you through some kind of personalization. Ask yourself: What do I want and why is it important to me? Quick results are required.

At the appointed time, you will take your place in a waiting area with a number of actors, many of whom will probably look a lot like you. Everyone is preparing, and chit chat is rare. At last you will be called into the room.

In a preliminary or "screening" audition, you will probably be reading with a single casting person. If your reading goes well, and if you seem right for the role, you may be asked to return for a callback, probably later that same day.

Outside of Los Angeles, and sometimes in it, a video camera will be used. You will be asked to "slate" yourself by saying your name and the role for which you are reading. Make good eye contact with the camera and speak clearly; let the people watching the tape know that you are a solid professional who enjoys the work. Then play the scene directly to the casting person who is reading with you. They will usually sit just beside the camera. Speak so that the microphone on the front of the camera can pick up your voice well, but don't falsify your performance.

At a callback in Los Angeles, you will enter the room and be introduced by the casting assistant to anywhere from three to seven people. These are the director, the casting director, and the producers. Though it can feel like a court martial, remember that these people are on your side, no matter how bored or distant they may seem. They want you to succeed, since that makes their job easier. On very rare occasions, the director or one of the producers may ask you to try the scene again with some adjustment. If this happens, don't get your hopes up; there's no telling whether it means that you have a better chance at the role or not. Just try to divest yourself of your preparation and experience the scene anew with the adjustment suggested.

If the callback is for a regular or recurring role in a sitcom or soap opera, you may go through several rounds of auditions. If you make it to the finals, your agent will make a "test deal" determining your salary and guaranteed number of episodes before the *network audition*. These are nerve-wracking affairs, and the room is full of people; in addition to a host of writer/producers, the production company and the network have sent their representatives as well.

Perhaps the greatest challenge in any of these audition situations is to really be there in the "here and now." Your first few auditions may seem like dreams, and you may come away with only a vague sense of what happened or who was there. When you get in the room, take a moment to breathe, to see where you are and who is there; treat it like a social situation in which you are glad to be present. Then, as you perform, go for it. Play the scene directly with the casting person who is reading the other character. No matter how terrible their performance may be (and it is usually pretty bad), make good contact with them by putting your objective into them. Try to affect them. Make the event live.

Don't be tied rigidly to your script, but don't ignore it either. It is better to be a bit rough on the lines but alive, than to be technically correct but mechanical. Don't try to create a character, just let yourself say and do what the character does with full commitment in your own voice and your own body. The auditioners want to get a good sense of you; they are looking for someone who brings an interesting quality to the role in their very presence before the camera. (The assumption, by the way, is that you will do on the set exactly what you did in the audition.) After any audition, the result will be communicated through your agent later that day. The actors who have been rejected are usually not notified, so no news is bad news.

Auditions are much more enjoyable if you approach them without a sense of competitiveness. Think of them not as a contest with other actors but as an opportunity to communicate your potential to a director or producer. Take the long view and remember that the opinion formed of you at an audition may be important at some future time, even if you don't get this particular part. Above all, do not take auditions personally. It usually requires many auditions before you will land a part. When you are starting out, it may take twenty or more. As hard as it may be, don't take every rejection as a reflection on your talent. Remember that auditions do not test your artistry so much as they test your usefulness for the specific role at hand. True, you have to eventually deliver the goods, but first you have to be in the right place at the right time.

It will be difficult at times; keep your sense of humor, share your feelings with friends. Remember that tenacity is required; a film or television career is very much a matter of persistence, and overnight success takes years.

Exercise 14.1: Auditions

Set up a simulated audition situation in your class. Distribute specific scenes and give yourselves about an hour to prepare. Then record the auditions, with one of you sitting beside the camera as the casting person reading (badly) the other part in the scene. Slate each audition. Watch and critique the results.

Summary

Beginning a film or television career is an all-consuming task. The critical first steps are finding a way to support yourself while simultaneously pursuing your career, developing a network of support, finding an agent, and eventually joining a union. The audition process is a difficult but necessary part of the actor's life and is best approached with the long view that each audition is an opportunity to establish yourself in the consciousness of those who hire. Remember that landing work is mostly a matter of persistence and of being in the right place at the right time, and rejection is not a reflection on your talent.

AFTERWORD

The Ethics of Film Acting

At the beginning of the twentieth century, Stanislavsky and others began an attempt to replace the nineteenth century tradition of overblown bravura acting with a new approach dedicated to psychological truthfulness, economy of means, and a commitment to the improvement of society. These ideals manifested themselves in many ways, in the work of many directors, teachers, and writers, and permanently changed the face of world theater.

It was not until the development of film and television as dramatic forms, however, that the opportunity arose to realize Stanislavsky's ideals to the fullest. The proximity of the camera and its ability to see into the inner world of the character make psychological truthfulness and economy of means not possibilities, but requirements. Perhaps more important, the vastness of the potential audience makes the possibility of influencing society—for good as well as for ill—real to an extent that those who run studios and networks (as well as directors, writers, and actors) are often afraid to contemplate, much less take responsibility for.

You must consider that your skill as an actor is a kind of power over others. Those whose skill gives them such power—doctors, lawyers, clergy—are called members of the "professional" class because they must *profess* an ethic: They must vow to use their skill only for the benefit of those they serve. You must take your acting skill as seriously. As hard as it may be to influence the work done by studios and networks, you must at least accept responsibility for the ways in which you allow your acting power to be used. You must develop a *sense of purpose*.

Your sense of purpose grows from your respect for your own talent, your love for the specific material you are performing, and your desire to use both to serve your audience. It is this drive to be *at service* through your art that will finally overcome the self-consciousness of your ego and carry you beyond yourself, giving you a transcendent purpose from which come dignity, fulfillment, and ongoing artistic vitality.

Stanislavsky called this ongoing artistic vitality "theatrical youthfulness." Near the end of his life he addressed a group of young actors who were entering the Moscow Art Theatre with these words:

> Yes, you must be excited about your profession. You must love it devotedly and passionately, but not for itself, not for its laurels, not for the pleasure and delight it brings to you as artists. You must love your chosen profession because it

119

gives you the opportunity to communicate ideas that are important and necessary to your audience. Because it gives you the opportunity, through the ideas that you dramatize on the stage and through your characterizations, to educate your audience and to make them better, finer, wiser, and more useful members of society.[1]

The art of acting has always had a very special service to render, one that has become increasingly important today: it is rooted in the actor's ability to transform, to become "someone else." At a time when the individual can feel insignificant and impotent, the actor's ability to be "in charge" of personal reality can be a source of hope and inspiration to others. The actor's ability to undergo transformation is itself a kind of potency, a kind of power over the future. While a play or a film may teach us something about who we are, it is the actor's ability to be transformed that teaches us something about who we may become by reminding us of our own capacity for self-definition.

As we enter the new millennium, we face an explosion of performance opportunities in the proliferation of cable and satellite TV, pre-recorded media, and the possibilities of the internet as an entertainment delivery system. The role of the actor can only expand, and the need for ethical and responsible behavior by everyone in the entertainment field can only increase. If you are willing to work in this spirit, you will find your horizons being continually broadened by a renewed sense of ethical and spiritual purpose. It can be a wonderful time to be an actor.

---

[1]Nikolai Gorchakov, *Stanislavsky Directs* (New York: Funk & Wagnalls, 1954), pp. 40–41.

APPENDIX A

Sample Scenes

From *Death of a Salesman* by Arthur Miller[1]

[After a life spent as a travelling salesman, Willy Loman is getting on in years. He is starting to fall asleep at the wheel, and can no longer safely cover his territory. He goes to see his new boss, who has recently inherited the business. Willy hopes to be assigned to a territory in town. Instead, he is fired. This sends Willy into a spiral of depression and desperation which impacts everyone in his family. At last, he commits suicide so that his family will receive his life insurance, thus earning his last "paycheck."]

> [*Howard Wagner, thirty-six . . . is intent on threading a recording machine and only glances over his shoulder as Willy appears.*]
>
> *Willy:*   Pst! Pst!
>
> *Howard:*   Hello, Willy, come in.
>
> *Willy:*   Like to have a little talk with you, Howard.
>
> *Howard:*   Sorry to keep you waiting. I'll be with you in a minute.
>
> *Willy:*   What's that, Howard?
>
> *Howard:*   Didn't you ever see one of these? Wire recorder.
>
> *Willy:*   Oh. Can we talk a minute?
>
> *Howard:*   Records things. Just got delivery yesterday. Been driving me crazy, the most terrific machine I ever saw in my life. I was up all night with it.
>
> *Willy:*   What do you do with it?
>
> *Howard:*   I bought it for dictation, but you can do anything with it. Listen to this. I had it home last night. Listen to what I picked up. The first one is my daughter. Get this. [*He flicks the switch and "Roll out the Barrel" is heard being whistled.*] Listen to that kid whistle.
>
> *Willy:*   Ts, ts. Like to ask a little favor if you . . .
>
> [*The whistling breaks off, and the voice of Howard's daughter is heard.*]

[1]From *Death of a Salesman* by Arthur Miller. Copyright © 1949, renewed © 1977 by Arthur Miller (Dramatists Play Service version used). Used by permission of Viking Penguin, a division of Penguin Books USA Inc.

His Daughter: "Now you, Daddy."

Howard: She's crazy for me! [*Again the same song is whistled.*] That's me! Ha! [*He winks.*]

Willy: You're very good!

[*The whistling breaks off again. The machine runs silent for a moment.*]

Howard: Sh! Get this now, this is my son.

His Son: "The capital of Alabama is Montgomery; the capital of Arizona is Phoenix; the capital of Arkansas is Little Rock; the capital of California is Sacramento . . ." [*and on, and on.*]

Howard, holding up five fingers: Five years old, Willy!

Willy: He'll make an announcer some day!

His Son, continuing: "The capital . . ."

Howard: Get that—alphabetical order! [*The machine breaks off suddenly.*] Wait a minute. The maid kicked the plug out.

Willy: It certainly is a—

Howard: Sh, for God's sake!

His Son: "It's nine o'clock, Bulova watch time. So I have to go to sleep."

Willy: That really is—

Howard: Wait a minute! The next is my wife.

[*They wait.*]

Howard's Voice: "Go on, say something." [*Pause.*] "Well, you gonna talk?"

His Wife, shyly, beaten: "Hello." [*Silence.*] "Oh, Howard, I can't talk into this . . ."

Howard, snapping the machine off: That was my wife.

Willy: That is a wonderful machine. Can we—

Howard: I tell you, *Willy,* I'm gonna take my camera, and my bandsaw, and all my hobbies, and out they go. This is the most fascinating relaxation I ever found.

Willy: I think I'll get one myself.

Howard: Sure, they're only a hundred and a half. You can't do without it. Supposing you wanna hear Jack Benny, see? But you can't be at home at that hour. So you tell the maid to turn the radio on when Jack Benny comes on, and this automatically goes on with the radio . . .

Willy: And when you come home you . . .

Howard: You can come home twelve o'clock, one o'clock, any time you like, and you get yourself a Coke and sit yourself down, throw the switch, and there's Jack Benny's program in the middle of the night!

Willy: I'm definitely going to get one. Because lots of time I'm on the road, and I think to myself, what I must be missing on the radio!

Howard: Don't you have a radio in the car?

Willy: Well, yeah, but who ever thinks of turning it on?

Howard: Say, aren't you supposed to be in Boston?

Willy: That's what I want to talk to you about, Howard. You got a minute? [*He draws a chair in from the wing.*]

Howard: What happened? What're you doing here?

Willy: Well . . .

Howard: You didn't crack up again, did you?

Willy: Oh, no. No . . .

Howard: Geez, you had me worried there for a minute. What's the trouble?

Willy: Well, tell you the truth, Howard. I've come to the decision that I'd rather not travel any more.

Howard: Not travel! Well, what'll you do?

Willy: Remember, Christmas time, when you had the party here? You said you'd try to think of some spot for me here in town.

Howard: With us?

Willy: Well, sure.

Howard: Oh, yeah, yeah. I remember. Well, I couldn't think of anything for you, Willy.

Willy: I tell ya, Howard. The kids are all grown up, y'know. I don't need much any more. If I could take home—well, sixty-five dollars a week, I could swing it.

Howard: Yeah, but Willy, see I—

Willy: I tell ya why, Howard. Speaking frankly and between the two of us, y'know—I'm just a little tired.

Howard: Oh, I could understand that, Willy. But you're a road man, Willy, and we do a road business. We've only got a half-dozen salesmen on the floor here.

Willy: God know, Howard, I never asked a favor of any man. But I was with the firm when your father used to carry you in here in his arms.

Howard: I know that, Willy, but—

Willy: Your father came to me the day you were born and asked me what I thought of the name Howard, may he rest in peace.

Howard: I appreciate that, Willy, but there just is no spot here for you. If I had a spot I'd slam you right in, but I just don't have a single solitary spot.

[He looks for his lighter. Willy has picked it up and gives it to him. Pause.]

Willy, with increasing anger: Howard, all I need to set my table is fifty dollars a week.

Howard: But where am I going to put you, kid?

Willy: Look, it isn't a question of whether I can sell merchandise, is it?

Howard: No, but it's a business, kid, and everybody's gotta pull his own weight.

WILLY, desperately: Just let me tell you a story, Howard—

Howard: 'Cause you gotta admit, business is business.

Willy, angrily: Business is definitely business, but just listen for a minute. You don't understand this. When I was a boy—eighteen, nineteen—I was already on the road. And there was a question in my mind as to whether selling had a future for me. Because in those days I had a yearning to go to Alaska. See, there were three gold strikes in one month in Alaska, and I felt like going out. Just for the ride you might say.

Howard, barely interested: Don't say.

Willy: Oh, yeah, my father lived many years in Alaska. He was an adventurous man. We've got quite a little streak of self-reliance in our family. I thought I'd go out with my older brother and try to locate him, and maybe settle in the North with the old man. And I was almost decided to go, when I met a sales man in the Parker House. His name was Dave Singleman. And he was eighty-four years old, and he'd drummed merchandise in thirty-one states. And old Dave, he'd go up to his room, y'understand, put on his green velvet slippers—I'll never forget—and pick up his phone and call the buyers, and without ever leaving his room, at the age of eighty-four, he made his living. And when I saw that, I realized that selling was the greatest career a man could want. 'Cause what could be more satisfying than to be able to go, at the age of eighty-four, into twenty or thirty different cities, and pick up a phone, and be remembered and loved and helped by so many different people? Do you know? when he died—and by the way he died the death of a salesman, in his green velvet slippers in the smoker of the New York, New Haven and Hartford, going into Boston—when he died, hundreds of salesmen and buyers were at his funeral. Things were sad on a lotta trains for months after that. *[He stands up. Howard has not looked at him.]* In those days there was personality in it, Howard. There was respect, and comradeship, and gratitude in it. Today, it's all cut and dried, and there's no chance for bringing friendship to bear—or personality. You see what I mean? They don't know me anymore.

Howard, moving away, to the right: That's just the thing, Willy.

Willy: If I had forty dollars a week—that's all I'd need. Forty dollars, Howard.

Howard: Kid, I can't take blood from a stone, I—

Willy, desperation is on him now: Howard, the year Al Smith was nominated, your father came to me and—

Howard, starting to go off: I've got to see some people, kid.

Willy, stopping him: I'm talking about your father! There were promises made across this desk! You mustn't tell me you've got people to see— I put thirty-four years into this firm, Howard, and now I can't pay my insurance! You can't eat the orange and throw the peel away—a man is not a piece of fruit! *[After a pause:]* Now pay attention. Your father—in 1928 I had a big year. I averaged a hundred and seventy dollars a week in commissions.

Howard, impatiently: Now, Willy, you never averaged—

Willy, banging his hand on the desk: I averaged a hundred and seventy dollars a week in the year of 1928! And your father came to me—or rather, I was in the office here—it was right over this desk—and he put his hand on my shoulder—

Howard, getting up: You'll have to excuse me, Willy, I gotta see some people. Pull yourself together. Going out: I'll be back in a little while.

[On Howard's exit, the light on his chair grows very bright and strange.]

Willy: Pull myself together! What the hell did I say to him? My God, I was yelling at him! How could I! *[Willy breaks off, staring at the light, which occupies the chair, animating it. He approaches this chair, standing across the desk from it.]* Frank, Frank, don't you remember what you told me that time? How you put your hand on my shoulder, and Frank . . . [He leans on the desk and as he speaks the dead man's name he accidentally switches on the recorder, and instantly]

Howard's Son: ". . . of New York is Albany. The capital of Ohio is Cincinnati, the capital of Rhode Island is . . ." [The recitation continues.]

Willy, leaping away with fright, shouting: Ha! Howard! Howard! Howard!

Howard, rushing in: What happened?

Willy, pointing at the machine, which continues nasally, childishly, with the capital cities: Shut it off! Shut it off!

Howard, pulling the plug out: Look, Willy . . .

Willy, pressing his hands to his eyes: I gotta get myself some coffee. I'll get some coffee . . .

[*Willy starts to walk out. Howard stops him.*]

Howard, rolling up the cord: Willy, look . . .

Willy: I'll go to Boston.

Howard: Willy, you can't go to Boston for us.

Willy: Why can't I go?

Howard: I don't want you to represent us. I've been meaning to tell you for a long time now.

Willy: Howard, are you firing me?

Howard: I think you need a good long rest, Willy.

Willy: Howard—

Howard: And when you feel better, come back, and we'll see if we can work something out.

Willy: But I gotta earn some money, Howard. I'm in no position to—

Howard: Where are your sons? Why don't your sons give you a hand?

Willy: They're working on a very big deal.

Howard: This is no time for false pride, Willy. You go to your sons and you tell them that you're tired. You've got two great boys, haven't you?

Willy: Oh, no question, no question, but in the meantime . . .

Howard: Then that's that, heh?

Willy: All right, I'll go to Boston tomorrow.

Howard: No, no.

Willy: I can't throw myself on my sons. I'm not a cripple!

Howard: Look, kid, I'm busy this morning.

Willy, grasping Howard's arm: Howard, you've got to let me go to Boston!

Howard, hard, keeping himself under control: I've got a line of people to see this morning. Sit down, take five minutes, and pull yourself together, and then go home, will ya? I need the office, Willy. [*He starts to go, turns, remembering the recorder, starts to push off the table holding the recorder.*] Oh, yeah. Whenever you can this week, stop by and drop off the samples. You'll feel better, Willy, and then come back and we'll talk. Pull yourself together, kid, there's people outside.

From *Miss Evers' Boys* by Walter Bernstein[1]

[It is 1942. Nurse Eunice Evers has been working for ten years at the all-black Tuskegee Hospital in a U.S. Public Health Service program to study syphilis in Negro males. When the Study began, syphilis was an incurable disease, but by 1942 penicillin has been shown to be an effective treatment. Two doctors are in charge of the Study: Dr. Douglas, a white doctor from Washington, and Dr. Brodus, an African-American. Both doctors refuse to allow the nearly 500 men under their care to receive penicillin, because doing so would invalidate the Study. Though Nurse Evers initially obeys the doctors, some of her patients begin to die; she finally steals some penicillin for one of the men. Unfortunately, he dies from drinking a home remedy. Evers, however, is afraid that she has caused his death, and gives in to the doctors. She remains with the Study until it is exposed and ended by a Senate investigating committee in 1972, 40 years after it began, when only 125 of the original 500 men are still alive.]

INT. TUSKEGEE HOSPITAL—BRODUS' OFFICE— DAY—1942

Miss Evers stands before Doctors Brodus and Douglas. Her face is set.

> MISS EVERS

They must have penicillin.

> DOUGLAS

I'm afraid we can't allow that.

> MISS EVERS

Why not? How long do those men have to wait? First in line, that's what you said . . . what you told me. That was the promise. Now, there's a drug—

> BRODUS

Penicillin can't undo the damage that's been done.

From *Miss Evers' Boys* by Walter Bernstein, based on the Play by David Feldshuh. Produced by Anasazi Productions in association with HBO NYC. Executive Producers Robert Benedetti and Laurence Fishburne, directed by Joseph Sargent. Courtesy of HBO.

MISS EVERS

It could keep them from getting worse.

DOUGLAS

It could also kill them.

MISS EVERS

Penicillin?

DOUGLAS

(nods)

Some chronic syphilitics have a fatal allergic reaction to penicillin . . . called the Herxheimer reaction. It's been proved. Washington is research-ing the question, to determine the degree of risk.

MISS EVERS

But they're giving it all over the state. Caleb Humphries got it, he's fine. He's in the goddamned Army!

She puts her hand to her mouth, aghast at the language she used.

MISS EVERS (CON'T.)

Excuse my language.

DOUGLAS

Caleb was lucky. Yes, penicillin is effective, in the primary and sec-ondary stages. But for those who have entered the tertiary stage, like the men in our study, it cannot cure, and it may kill! No, for them, the Study has to go to end point.

BRODUS

We already have ten years of data—

DOUGLAS

Ten years is not end point.

MISS EVERS

Then what is?

DOUGLAS

Autopsy. Our facts have to be validated by autopsy. That is the end point, Nurse Evers—autopsy. That will make it science, not guesswork.

MISS EVERS

(aghast)

We have to wait until they die?

DOUGLAS

Regrettable, but necessary. Science is sometimes a hard taskmaster, Nurse Evers. Do you think I like not treating them? But we must complete the Study! We have a chance here to make *history!*

MISS EVERS

(exploding, in tears)

History is people!

(She rushes from the room. Douglas looks to Brodus.)

BRODUS

Let me talk to her.

Brodus goes after Nurse Evers.

From *Cheers* by Tom Reeder[1]

[Carla works as a waitress in the Cheers bar. She has just received an offer of marriage from Ben Ludlow, an eminent psychologist she has been dating. She has reacted strangely to the proposal and has gone into the back room to think. Her boss, Diane, follows to see what's wrong.]

INT. POOL ROOM
Carla is standing lost in thought. *Diane enters.*

DIANE

Carla, I couldn't help noticing that you're not exactly leaping for joy. Bennett Ludlow is a wonderful catch.

CARLA

(WITH DIFFICULTY) There are things he doesn't know about me.

DIANE

A little mystery is good for a marriage. What haven't you told him?

CARLA

Well, I haven't been completely honest about my kids.

DIANE

What haven't you told him about them?

---

[1]From "Whodunit," by Tom Reeder, *Cheers* Episode #60593-057, 1984. Used by permission of Paramount Pictures Corporation.

CARLA

That they live.

DIANE

He doesn't know you have children?

CARLA

Shhhhh!

DIANE

Carla, you have to tell him. He's going to wonder who those little people are running around the house.

CARLA

I'm hoping he'll be too polite to ask.

OFF DIANE'S LOOK.

CARLA (CONT'D)

I didn't want to scare him off.

DIANE

Seriously, Carla, it's only fair that you tell him immediately that you have five children.

CARLA

Six.

DIANE

Okay, six. But if you wait, if you put this off—I thought it was five.

CARLA

It was. But I just came from the doctor.

DIANE GROANS WITH RECOGNITION.

DIANE

Carla, when you took hygiene in high school, did you cut the "how-not-to" lecture?

CARLA

I had to. I was pregnant. I tell you I'm the most fertile woman who ever lived. For me there's only one method of birth control that's absolutely foolproof, but it makes me sick to my stomach.

DIANE

What's that?

CARLA

Saying no.

LUDLOW ENTERS.

LUDLOW

Carla, are you all right?

DIANE

Well, I'm going to go celebrate with the others. We're like a big family here at Cheers. You know what they say about a big family—more to love. I always say—

CARLA

Beat it.

DIANE

Bye.

DIANE EXITS.

LUDLOW

Carla, my proposal wasn't received with the enthusiasm I expected it to be. In fact, it occurred to me that I never actually heard you say "yes."

CARLA

I know. Benny, I have to tell you some things about myself.

LUDLOW

This sounds serious.

CARLA

It is. Benny, have you ever seen "The Brady Bunch?"

LUDLOW

Yes, I think so.

CARLA

Picture them with knives.

LUDLOW

I don't understand.

CARLA

I have five children.

LUDLOW

Five?

CARLA

Well . . . five and counting. You're going to be a daddy.

LUDLOW SITS DOWN.

LUDLOW

This is quite a day.

CARLA

You now have my permission to withdraw the proposal.

LUDLOW

Do you want me to withdraw the proposal, Carla?

CARLA

I want you to do what you want to do.

LUDLOW

I want to marry you.

CARLA

You're kidding. Wow. What class.

LUDLOW

I still haven't heard you say yes.

CARLA

I know. (GENUINELY PUZZLED) Why do you think that is?

LUDLOW

I think if you examine your feelings, you'll know.

CARLA

Yeah, I guess I know. I love somebody else.

LUDLOW

Who?

CARLA

I don't know his name. I haven't met him yet, but I've had this real clear picture of him in my mind for what seems like forever. He's going to walk into this bar some night. Actually, not walk. More like swagger. You know, confidant but not cocky. He's okay-looking, but he's no pretty boy. He's a swell dresser. He's wearing this burgundy leather jacket. His nose is broken in all the right places. He's got this scar on his chin he won't talk about. He cracks his knuckles all the time. Drives me up the wall, but, what can you do? Doesn't talk much. Doesn't have to. He falls for me hard. I hurt him a few times. He gets over it. We get married.

SHE TURNS TO LUDLOW.

CARLA (CONT'D)

So you see, it would be kind of messy if I was already married when he gets here.

LUDLOW

You know something, Carla? I sort of have a dream girl myself.

CARLA

What's she like?

LUDLOW

She's a spunky, hearty, little curly-haired spitfire, who doesn't know what's good for her.

CARLA

I hope you find her some day.

LUDLOW

Me too. And I want you to know I intend to take care of this child financially.

CARLA

You bet your buns you will, Benny Baby.

HE EXITS. CARLA STANDS THERE CONSIDERING HER FATE.

APPENDIX B

Useful Scene Sources

The following are good sources of scenes with the qualities most useful for this book. Most are available in bookstores and on the internet. Publishers of plays are indicated when inexpensive paperback "acting editions" are available.

Screenplays

Apartment, The by Billy Wilder (Faber & Faber)

Big Lebowski, The by Ethan Coen et al. (Faber & Faber)

Birdcage, The by Elaine May (Newmarket Press)

Chasing Amy by Kevin Smith (Talk Miramax Books)

Chinatown by Robert Towne (Grove Press)

Clerks by Kevin Smith (Talk Miramax Books)

Dancing at Lughnasa by Frank McGuinnes, Brian Friel (Faber & Faber)

Dead Man Walking by Tim Robbins (Newmarket Press)

English Patient, The by Anthony Minghella et al. (Talk Miramax Books)

Fargo by Ethan Coen, Joel Coen (Faber & Faber)

Five Corners by John Patrick Shanley (Grove Press)

Four Weddings and a Funeral by Richard Curtis (St. Martin's Press)

Good Will Hunting by Matt Damon et al. (Talk Miramax Books)

Happiness by Todd Solondz (Faber & Faber)

Jackie Brown by Quentin Tarentino, Elmore Leaonard (Talk Miramax Books)

Joe Versus the Volcano by John Patrick Shanley (Grove Press)

L.A. Story by Steve Martin (Grove Press)

Last Detail, The by Robert Towne (Grove Press)

Life Less Ordinary, A by John Hodge (Faber & Faber)

Lost Highway by David Lynch (Faber & Faber)

Michael Collins by Neil Jordan (Plume)

Men in Black by Ed Solomon et al. (Newmarket Press)

Madness of King George, The by Alan Bennett (Random House)

Moonstruck by John Patrick Shanley (Grove Press)

Notting Hill by Richard Curtis et al. (Trafalgar Square)

Oscar and Lucinda by Laura Jones (Faber & Faber)

Piano, The by Jane Campion (Talk Miramax Books)

Player, The by Michael Tolkin (Grove Press)

Rounders by David Levien, Brian Koppleman (Hyperion Books)

Roxanne by Steve Martin (Grove Press)

Sense and Sensibility by Emma Thompson et al. (Newmarket Press)

Shakespeare in Love by Marc Norman, Tom Stoppard (Hyperion)

Shawshank Redemption, The by Frank Darabont (Newmarket Press)

Shine by Jan Sardi, Scott Hicks (Grove Press)

Slam by Richard Stratton, Kim Wozencraft (W.W. Norton & Co.)

Sling Blade by Billy Bob Thornton (Talk Miramax Books)

Smoke Signals by Sherman Alexie (Talk Miramax Books)

Snow Falling on Cedars by Ron Bass, Scott Hicks (Newmarket Press)

Stalag 17 by Billy Wilder (University of California Press)

Sunset Boulevard by Billy Wilder (University of California Press)

Swingers by Jon Favreau, Vince Vaughn (Talk Miramax Books)

Thelma and Louise by Callee Khouri (Grove Press)

Titanic by James Cameron (HarperCollins)

Truman Show, The by Andrew Niccol, Peter Weir

Wilde by Julian Mitchell et al. (Newmarket Press)

Plays

Absence of War by David Hare

After the Fall by Arthur Miller (Dramatists Play Service)

Ah, Wilderness! by Eugene O'Neill (Samuel French)

Albertine, in Five Times by Michel Tremblay

All My Sons by Arthur Miller (Dramatists Play Service)

Amen Corner, The by James Baldwin (Samuel French)

American Buffalo by David Mamet (Samuel French)

Andersonville Trial, The by Saul Levitt (Dramatists Play Service)

And Miss Reardon Drinks a Little by Paul Zindel (Dramatists Play Service)

Angels in America: Parts I and II by Tony Kushner (Theatre Communications Group)

Anna Christie by Eugene O'Neill (Vintage Books)

Arcadia by Tom Stoppard

Balm in Gilead by Lanford Wilson

Bedrooms: Five Comedies by Renee Taylor and Joseph Bolgna (Samuel French)

Bent by Martin Sherman (Samuel French)

Birdbath by Leonard Melfi (Samuel French)

Brighton Beach Memoirs by Neil Simon

Born Yesterday by Garson Kanin (Dramatists Play Service)

Career Girls by Mike Leigh

Caretaker, The by Harold Pinter

Cat on a Hot Tin Roof by Tennessee Williams (Dramatists Play Service)

Cell Mates by Simon Gray

Ceremonies in Dark Old Men by Lonne Elder III

Chapter Two by Neil Simon (Samuel French)

Chase, The by Horton Foote (Dramatists Play Service)

Children's Hour, The by Lillian Hellman (Dramatists Play Service)

Cloud Nine by Caryl Churchill

Colored Museum, The by George C. Wolfe (Broadway Play Publishing)

Come Back, Little Sheba by William Inge (Samuel French)

Come Back to the 5 & Dime, Jimmy Dean, Jimmy Dean by Ed Graczyk (Samuel French)

Comedians by Trevor Griffiths

Coupla White Chicks Sitting Around Talking, A by John Ford Noonan (Samuel French)

Crimes of the Heart by Beth Henley (Dramatists Play Service)

Crossing Delancey by Susan Sandler (Samuel French)

Crucible, The by Arthur Miller (Dramatists Play Service)

Dark at the Top of the Stairs, The by William Inge (Dramatists Play Service)

Day in the Death of Joe Egg, A by Peter Nichols (Samuel French)

Death and the Maiden by Ariel Dorfman

Death of a Salesman by Arthur Miller (Dramatists Play Service)

Death of Bessie Smith, The by Edward Albee (Plume)

Delicate Balance, A by Edward Albee (Samuel French)

Dejavu by John Osborne

Division Street by Steve Tesich (Samuel French)

Driving Miss Daisy by Alfred Uhry

Duet for One by Tom Kempinski (Samuel French)

Eccentricities of a Nightingale, The by Tennessee Williams (Dramatists Play Service)

Ecstasy of Rita Joe by George Ryga

Effect of Gamma Rays on Man-in-the-Moon Marigolds by Paul Zindel (Bantam)

Enter Laughing by Joseph Stein (Samuel French)

Extremities by William Mastrosimone (Samuel French)

Fences by August Wilson (Samuel French)

Fool for Love by Sam Shepard (Dramatists Play Service)

Frankie and Johnny in the Clair de Lune by Terrence McNally (Dramatists Play Service)

Gingerbread Lady, The by Neil Simon (Samuel French)

Glass Menagerie, The by Tennessee Williams (Dramatists Play Service)

Glengarry Glen Ross by David Mamet (Samuel French)

Golden Boy by Clifford Odets (Dramatists Play Service)

Hatful of Rain, A by Michael Vincente Gazzo (Samuel French)

Heidi Chronicles, The by Wendy Wasserstein (Dramatists Play Service)

House of Blue Leaves, The by John Guare (Samuel French)

Immigrant, The by Mark Harelik (Broadway Play Publishing)

I Never Sang for my Father by Robert Anderson (Dramatists Play Service)

I Ought to be in Pictures by Neil Simon (Samuel French)

It Had to be You by Renee Taylor and Joseph Bologna (Samuel French)

Joe Turner's Come and Gone by August Wilson

Jumpers by Tom Stoppard

Kiss of the Spider Woman by Manuel Puig

Last of the Red Hot Lovers by Neil Simon

Last Summer at Bluefish Cove by Jane Chambers (JH Press)

Laundry and Bourbon by James McLure (Dramatists Play Service)

Lie of the Mind, A by Sam Shepard (Dramatists Play Service)

Love in Vain: A Vision of Robert Johnson by Alan Greenberg

Life in the Theatre, A by David Mamet

Little Foxes, The by Lillian Hellman (Dramatists Play Service)

Long Day's Journey into Night by Eugene O'Neill (Yale University Press)

Look Homeward, Angel by Ketti Frings (Samuel French)

Lost in Yonkers by Neil Simon (Samuel French)

Lovers and Other Strangers by Renee Taylor and Joseph Bologna (Samuel French)

Luv by Murray Schisgal (Dramatists Play Service)

Ma Rainey's Black Bottom by August Wilson

Madman and the Nun, The by Stanislaw Witkiewicz

Marvin's Room by Scott McPherson

Master Class by Terrence McNally

Member of the Wedding by Carson McCullers

Miracle Worker, The by William Gibson

Master Harold and the Boys by Athol Fugard

Matchmaker, The by Thornton Wilder (Samuel French)

Middle Ages, The by A. R. Gurney, Jr. (Dramatists Play Service)

Moon for the Misbegotten, A by Eugene O'Neill (Samuel French)

Moonchildren by Michael Weller (Samuel French)

Murder at the Howard Johnson's by Ron Clark and Sam Bobrick (Samuel French)

My Dinner with Andre by Wallace Shawn, Andre Gregory

Nerd, The by Larry Shue (Dramatists Play Service)

'Night, Mother by Marsha Norman (Dramatists Play Service)

Night of the Iguana, The by Tennessee Williams (Dramatists Play Service)

No Exit by Jean Paul Sartre

No Place to be Somebody by Charles Gordone (Samuel French)

Odd Couple, The (Female Version) by Neil Simon (Samuel French)

Odd Couple, The (Male Version) by Neil Simon (Samuel French)

Of Mice and Men by John Steinbeck (Dramatists Play Service)

Oh Dad, Poor Dad, Mamma's Hung You in the Closet and I'm Feelin' So Sad by Arthur Kopit (Samuel French)

Old Times by Harold Pinter

Only Game in Town, The by Frank D. Gilroy (Samuel French)

On the Open Road by Steve Tesich (Samuel French)

Philadelphia Story, The by Philip Barry (Samuel French)

Picasso at the Lapin Agile by Steve Martin

Picnic by William Inge (Dramatists Play Service)

Prisoner of Second Avenue, The by Neil Simon (Samuel French)

Rainmaker, The by N. Richard Nash (Samuel French)

Raisin in the Sun, A by Lorraine Hansberry (Samuel French)

Red Coat, The by John Patrick Shanley (Dramatists Play Service)

Red Noses by Peter Barnes

Rosencrantz and Guildenstern Are Dead by Tom Stoppard

Scenes from American Life by A. R. Gurney, Jr. (Samuel French)

Sea Horse, The by Edward J. Moore (Samuel French)

Sexual Perversity in Chicago by David Mamet (Samuel French)

Shadow Box, The by Michael Cristofer (Samuel French)

Sign in Sidney Brustein's Window, The by Lorraine Hansberry (Samuel French)

Six Degrees of Separation by John Guare (Dramatists Play Service)

Speed-the-Plow by David Mamet (Samuel French)

Splendor in the Grass by William Inge (Dramatists Play Service)

Spoils of War by Michael Weller (Samuel French)

Steel Magnolias by Robert Harling (Dramatists Play Service)

Strange Snow by Stephen Metcalfe (Samuel French)

Streetcar Named Desire, A by Tennessee Williams (Dramatists Play Service)

Subject was Roses, The by Frank D. Gilroy (Samuel French)

Summer and Smoke by Tennessee Williams (Dramatists Play Service)

Sweet Bird of Youth by Tennessee Williams (Dramatists Play Service)

Tenth Man, The by Paddy Chayefsky (Samuel French)

That Championship Season by Jason Miller (Samuel French)

Time of Your Life, The by William Saroyan (Samuel French)

To Gillian on her 37th Birthday by Michael Brady (Broadway Play Publishing)

Touch of the Poet, A by Eugene O'Neill (Random House)

Toys in the Attic, by Lillian Hellman (Dramatists Play Service)

Tribute by Bernard Slade (Samuel French)

True West by Sam Shepard (Samuel French)

Twice Around the Park by Murray Schisgal (Samuel French)

View from the Bridge, A by Arthur Miller (Dramatists Play Service)

Vikings by Stephen Metcalfe (Samuel French)

Waiting for Lefty by Clifford Odets (Grove Press)

Welcome to the Dollhouse by Todd Solondz

What I Did Last Summer by A. R. Gurney, Jr. (Dramatists Play Service)

When You Comin' Back, Red Ryder? By Mark Medoff (Dramatists Play Service)

Who's Afraid of Virginia Woolf? By Edward Albee (Dramatists Play Service)

Women, The by Clare Boothe Luce (Dramatists Play Service)

Zoo Story, The by Edward Albee (Dramatists Play Service)

Useful Collections

Best American Short Plays, 1993–1994, ed. Howard Stein, Glenn Young

Best American Short Plays, 1995–1996, ed. Howard Stein, Glenn Young

Between Worlds: Contemporary Asian-American Plays, ed. Misha Berson

But Still, Like Air, I'll Rise: New-Asian American Plays, ed. Velina Hasu Houston

By Southern Playwrights, ed. Michael Bigelow

Decade of New Comedy, A, Vol. I and II, ed. Michael Bigelow

Great Scenes from Minority Playwrights, ed. Marsh Cassady, Theodore O. Zapel

Great Scenes from Women Playwrights, ed. Marsh Cassady, Theodore O. Zapel

Jelly's Last Jam, ed. George C. Wolfe

Luis Valdez: Early Works, by Luis Valdez

Multicultural Theatre: Vol. I and II, ed. Roger Ellis

TV Scenes for Actors, ed. Sigmund A. Stoler, Arthur L. Zopel

Voices of Color, ed. Woodie King, Jr.

GLOSSARY OF FILM AND TELEVISION TERMS

Abby Singer   The next-to-the-last shot of the day.

Action   What happens in a scene or story; what a character does to pursue an objective; what the director calls to start a shot.

AD, First   The director's right-hand person, in charge of all logistics on the set.

AD, Second   The second assistant director is in charge of personnel, including the placement and timing of all extras in background action. There is also a second second who handles paperwork. All ADs are distinguished by their walkie-talkies.

ADR   Automatic Dialogue Replacement, a process whereby dialogue from the production sound track is replaced. Also called "looping."

AEA   The Actors Equity Association, which has jurisdiction over live theater.

AFTRA   The American Federation of Radio and Television Artists, which has jurisdiction over radio and many shows shot in video.

Agent   The actor's representative who submits the actor for roles and makes all deals; must be franchised by the unions. Receives a straight commission of 10 percent as the only pay for services.

Angle   The position and view of the camera.

Aspect Ratio   The proportion (ratio of height to width) of the screen on which the show will be projected. The "Academy" ratio is 1.33 to 1 and was once the standard for movies. It was adopted for television, though television cuts off a margin on all sides of a film frame. Feature films and hi-definition television are wider, 1.85 to 1, and Cinemascope and Panavision are wider yet, 2.35 to 1.

Background   The people and things that complete the environment, including extras, animals, and vehicles.

Bell   The signal that a take is ready to be made.

Best Boy   The person in charge of electrical equipment.

Big Close-up   The closest shot, face only; also called *ECU* (Extreme Close-up).

Blocking   The positions of the actors in sequence throughout the scene, each marked on the floor with tape.

Board   The arrangement of scenes in the order to shot.

Boom   A pole on which a microphone is suspended over the heads of the actors.

Breakdown   A list of roles to be cast with brief descriptions sent to agents by the casting director.

Call   The time of day the actor is to report for work.

Callback   A final stage in the casting process when a final selection is made for a role from among a few actors.

Call Sheet   The shooting orders for the following day distributed at the end of each day's shooting.

Camera Operator   The head of the camera crew who frames the shots.

Camera Right or Left   The direction of the actor movements as seen from the camera.

Casting Director   The person who handles all the logistics of the casting process; they suggest actors, conduct auditions, and make the deal when an actor is hired.

Check the Gate   After a scene has been shot, the camera assistant makes sure there was nothing in the mechanism of the camera which could ruin the film.

Cheating   An adjustment in position, look, or movement by the actor for the sake of the camera's perspective or movement.

Clapper Board   the board which is photographed at the start of each take to identify the shot and to establish sound synchronization by the "clapping" of a stick.

Close-up   A tight shot, neck up.

Close Shot   A "medium close-up," chest up.

Company   All the people working on the show. When they have to move, it is a "company move."

Continuity   The smooth flow of shots and scenes with no disruptions by incorrect details. The script supervisor has the main responsibility for this during shooting.

Cover Set   An indoor location which is used in place of an outdoor set in case of bad weather.

Coverage   The closer shots taken in a scene to be inserted into the master.

Cross   A move by an actor from one position to another.

Cue Cards   Cards showing an actor's lines, held on the actor's eye-line.

Cut   A version of the show as edited; the sequence is usually rough cut, director's cut, producer's cut, final cut. Also what the director calls to stop a take.

DGA   The Director's Guild of America.

DOOD   Day-Out-of-Days, a chart showing when each actor works and correlates the days of shooting with the days of the week and month.

DP   The director of photography, sometimes called a cinematographer; along with the director, responsible for the "look" of the show including lighting and camera placement.

Dailies   The footage shot the previous day which has been processed and sent to the set and production company for viewing by the director and producers.

Day   Whenever the action of the story moves into a new period, it is a "day." The script days are numbered consecutively no matter how much time elapses between them, as Day One, Day Two, etc.

Day Player   An actor in a smaller role, usually paid by the day, although these parts can sometimes work for weeks.

Depth of Field   The narrow range in which the camera's subject is in perfect focus.

Dolly Grip   The camera crew member in charge of moving the camera.

Double   Also an actor who replaces another, as in stunt double or photo double; also when more than one piece of wardrobe is supplied in case the first is ruined.

Downstage   Toward the camera.

Dressing   The things on the set that create a complete sense of a real place.

Drive-To   A location close enough to the home city that accommodations are not provided by the company.

Dubbing   Mixing the various sound elements—dialogue, effects and music—to accompany the picture. Also called the *Final Mix.*

Dubbing Stage   The facility in which the picture can be projected while the accompanying sound elements are mixed.

ECU   Extreme close-up: also called *Big Close-up.*

Equity   See AEA.

Establishing Shot   A view of a place which is used to tell the audience where they are.

Eye Line   The placement of the actor's eyes as he or she looks at someone off-camera.

Extras   The people who round out the environment; also called *Background.*

Favor   When the camera position throws more emphasis to one character over another.

First AD   See *AD.*

First Position   The position of each actor as the scene begins.

First Team   The principal actors.

Final Cut   See *Cut.* What every director dreams of having.

Final Mix   See *Dubbing.*

First Assembly   The first compilation of the show with the scenes in order; also called a rough cut, or editor's cut.

Floor Manager   In television, the director's representative on the floor.

Focus Puller   The member of the camera team in charge of focus.

Foley   The footsteps and other sound effects that must synchronize with the picture.

Gaffer   The DP's right-hand person, in charge of the lighting crew. The best boy is the gaffer's right hand person.

Green Light   Approval to go into production.

Grip   A person in charge of moving equipment such as lights or sets. Named after the bag of tools which they used to carry.

Hero Prop   A prop with special importance often needing special handling by the actor.

Hi-Def   High definition digital video. May someday replace film.

Hitting a Mark   Taking the proper position.

Key   A crew chief; also the principal light source in a scene.

Line-Up   When the director, DP and actors go through a scene to establish camera positions.

Line Producer   The producer who handles the details and logistics of the entire company and shoot. Similar to, but a notch above, a unit production manager.

Local Casting Director   Handles casting in the area where a film is to shoot.

Local Hire   An actor or crew member hired locally when on location.

Location   One of the places in which the show will be shot.

Locking the Cut   The point after which no further changes in the visual aspects of the show will be made.

Look   The appearance of the show.

Looping   See ADR and walla.

Long Shot   A distant or wide camera position.

MOW   Movie of the Week, or movie made for television.

Marks   The position of each actor marked by tape on the floor.

Martini   The last shot of the day.

Master   The most inclusive view of a scene, usually shot first.

Matching   When one thing can be cut to another without disruption.

Mike   Microphone.

Moving On   Going on to the next scene.

Music Editor   Works with the composer and prepares the recordings from the scoring session for use in the final mix.

New Deal   Moving on to the next scene.

On a Bell   When the set is "locked down" during shooting.

On Hold   When an actor is actually not scheduled to work, but must be quickly available in case they are needed.

On Location   Working away from the sound stage or away from the home city.

One-Liner   A short version of the shooting schedule.

PA   Production assistant. These people usually wear walkie-talkies and do whatever needs doing on the set.

Pickup   A portion of a scene to be reshot.

Post   The post-production period during which the film is edited and the sound elements are added.

Prelay   The advance preparation of sound elements such as sound effects, dialogue, etc.

Prep   Getting ready to shoot a film.

Principal Photography   The main shooting period of a film.

Print It   What the director tells the script supervisor when he or she wants a shot to appear on the dailies; may also signal that work on a shot is done, though not always.

Production Track   The sound recorded when the show was shot.

Prop   Anything handled by the actors during a scene.

Prop Master   The person in charge of all props.

Radio Mike   A microphone hidden in the actor's clothes which broadcasts to a receiver nearby.

Rainbow   The shooting script with all its changed colored pages in place.

Reshoot   Redoing a portion of a film after principal photography has ended.

Roll It   The call from the first AD to start the sound recorder, answered by the call of "speed" when the production sound mixer is recording.

Rolling   When the camera is running; everyone on the set must be absolutely quiet.

SAG   The Screen Actors Guild, the union with jurisdiction over film actors.

Second Unit   A small camera team which shoots material which does not involve principal actors, such as establishing shots.

Scoring Session   The recording of the music for a film.

Scout   A visit to a location to plan the work to be done there.

Script Supervisor   The person in charge of continuity, and remembering every detail of every shot. They also prepare a script that shows how each line was covered and what the nature of each shot was; this is invaluable to the editor. An unsung hero.

Second AD   See AD.

Second Team   The stand-ins who substitute for the first team while the lighting is done.

Set   Where a scene is being shot, whether it is a real place or was built.

Setup   A camera position and all the attendant lighting, laying of track, etc.

Shoot   The period of actual production.

Shooting Schedule   A detailed list of sequence of the scenes to be shot and everything needed for each.

Shooting Script   The script as prepared for shooting, marked with the scenes numbered consecutively.

Shot   One segment of a scene from one camera angle.

Shot List   The list of shots each camera in a three-camera show is to make; in single-camera film, a list some directors supply for the work to be done that day, shot by shot.

Shot Size   The relative distance of the camera which determines exactly what the edges of the frame are.

Sides   The half-size pages of script distributed each day, containing the scenes to be shot that day.

Single   A shot containing only one actor.

Sitcom   A situation comedy.

Slate   The identification of a scene by photographing a board with the necessary information just before the shot begins. See also *Clapper Board.*

Soap Opera   More politely called daytime dramas.

Sound Mixer   The production sound mixer; there are also sound mixers who do the re-recording of the show with sound effects and music in the final mix.

Sound Stage   A special building designed for film production.

Speed   See *Roll It.*

Spotting   Locating where the sound effects and music will go in the locked cut.

Stage Right or Left   Movement from the actor's perspective as they face the camera.

Supervising Sound Editor   The person who oversees the sound mixing process, including selecting material for ADR, supervising the prelays, source music, and so on.

Take   A version of a shot.

Taping   The final performance of a sitcom, usually with a live audience.

Technical Director   In multiple-camera shows, the person who actually switches from shot to shot.

Teleprompter   A monitor that shows an actor's lines; see *Cue Cards.*

Turnaround   The time off which must be guaranteed to an actor or crew member between work days; different in various situations.

Two-shot   A shot of two actors.

Tracking   Moving the camera to follow the action, often on an actual track.

Underscore   The old-fashioned term for the music which accompanies a film.

UPM   Unit production manager; see *Line Producer.*

Upstage   Away from the camera.

Video Assist   A video feed coming directly from the camera lens which can be viewed on a monitor during shooting.

Walla   Adding the human sounds, such as crowd noises and telephone voices that complete the environment. This is the business of *looping groups.*

Warm-Up Person   A person who entertains the audience at a sitcom taping between takes.

Wild Lines   Lines of dialogue recorded without picture for possible use by the editor.

Wrap   The end of work, be it for a day or the entire picture.

INDEX

Note: This index does not duplicate the general topics listed in the subheadings of the Contents; I recommend that you look there first for general topics. Two-word entries are alphabetized under the first word; for example, "Camera operator" rather than "Operator, camera."

151